SEEKING A
Life
THAT COUNTS

SEEKING A
Life
THAT COUNTS

FINDING TRUE HAPPINESS
A STUDY OF ECCLESIASTES

G. SCOTT GLEAVES

Gospel Advocate Company
Nashville, Tennessee

Published by Gospel Advocate Co.
1006 Elm Hill Pike, Nashville, TN 37210
http://www.gospeladvocate.com

ISBN: 0-89225-555-2

ACKNOWLEDGMENTS

I'm grateful to God for my wife, Sherri, who inspires me with her love, humor and spiritual commitment. God has also blessed me with three children: Lindsay, Nathan and Taylor. I serve a loving congregation that patiently supports my efforts at writing, teaching and preaching God's marvelous Word.

Many people have assisted me in the writing of this book, and some deserve special recognition for their encouragement, editorial skills and constructive criticism: Pat Hogan, Dr. Scott Sutterfield, Paula Alford and Carol Bankirer.

I serve God under the oversight of five godly elders of the Lord's church: Bob Mullinax, Walt Driver, Lamar Evers, Jimmy Sullivan and Don Covan. These men have had a profound impact upon my life. In appreciation for them and for my fellow Christians in Tallahassee, Fla., I dedicate this book to my brethren at the Timberlane Church of Christ.

TABLE OF CONTENTS

INTRODUCTION

Are you tired of the gimmicks, the scams and the shallow answers to your difficult questions? In our world, much that passes as intelligence is superficial. Linda, a member of the church where I serve as minister, received the news that she had breast cancer. Linda was a single mom with three wonderful girls and an increasing awareness of the brevity of life. Over the years she had been riding a roller-coaster of emotions. She was in and out of the hospital, and in recent years the cancer reappeared in other places in her body. A spot on her brain was discovered, and in a matter of weeks she was dead.

When I began my work with the Timberlane congregation, I was introduced to Linda. As I sat in her home talking with her, she asked some difficult questions. "Why am I suffering so much?" she asked, her eyes hinting at despair. "What will happen to my kids? Who will care for them? How can I live with all the pain and nausea?" Hard questions. What would you say? How would you try to comfort her and help her see a reason to fight for her life? What could you say that would give her hope?

My training and education had not prepared me for ministering to people who face some of the most difficult challenges in life. However, I discovered a technique for facing life with courage. It was not a newly published how-to book but an ancient book of wisdom that is honest about life's enigmas. The book is found in the Old Testament and bears the name Ecclesiastes. Contained in its pages are many of the answers a person may seek. You will not find in it superficiality or shallowness. You will find real answers to tough questions. The book of Ecclesiastes deals honestly and forthrightly with life. I must caution you, however, before you embark on a study of the book to brace yourself because the author is blunt and sometimes caustic. You may not like how he gets his point across, but you will love the truthfulness of his message.

Linda lives on as an inspiration to all who knew her. Despite her fears, her pain and her doubts, she never lost her way or ever stopped living for God. She knew what was real and what was a facade. She embraced the words of the book of Ecclesiastes and never wavered or departed from them. She may have had a short life, but her life was full nonetheless. She had found happiness and contentment. The book of Ecclesiastes offers you the same deal. God has given you a realistic approach to happiness in the book of Ecclesiastes. If you want to be happy, keep reading. The journey will be worth it!

Dr. G. Scott Gleaves
Tallahassee, Fla.

1

SEEKING HAPPINESS, FINDING MISERY

*We are dying, we are dying, piecemeal our bodies
are dying and our strength leaves us, and our soul
cowers naked in the dark rain over the flood, cowering
in the last branches of the tree of our life.*
– D.H. Lawrence, The Ship of Death (1932)

*So I hated life, for the work which had been done under the
sun was grievous to me; because everything is futility and
striving after wind (Ecclesiastes 2:17).*

Ken sat at the bar, his glassy eyes gazing toward oblivion. He wasn't looking at anything in particular, just daydreaming. His eyes shifted downward toward the glass of whiskey sitting on the bar. With feelings of depression and despair, he reached for the glass, then slowly withdrew his hand. Ken felt that his life was as empty as if he were floating aimlessly on the ocean's surface with no sense of direction or purpose. He had been raised in a good home. He had a promising career in the military, but something was missing. He was getting weary of the same old routine of life. Even the alcohol bored him.

As Ken sat there, elbows firmly planted, he remembered the days when he read the Bible as a young boy. Ken hadn't bothered to read it much in recent years. After all, how could such an old book help him? Ken glanced toward some dusty shelves in a dark corner of the room. To his surprise, he saw what he thought might be a Bible. He walked over and pulled it from the shelf. He moved the glass aside and placed the dusty Bible in front of him. Upon opening it, he stumbled onto a verse that read, " 'Vanity of vanities,' says the Preacher, 'Vanity of vanities! All is vanity.' " Ken's eyes stayed glued to the pages as he read and absorbed the entire book of Ecclesiastes.

Ken's life changed that day. Realizing he was going nowhere, he recommitted his life to Jesus. Several years later, Ken became a deacon in the Lord's church with aspirations to teach people about having a life with God. Today, he is an enthusiastic church leader and a man with real meaning and purpose in life. If you were to ask Ken about what changed him, without hesitation he would attribute the change to the message of Ecclesiastes. My experience with many people who have read Ecclesiastes is much the same.

Ecclesiastes has been the subject of fierce debate since it was written. The nature of its content affects readers in one of two ways. People are either drawn to it or repelled by it. Why is this book so different from the other books in the Old Testament? Why would God give the world a book of this type? And to what end does its message serve? These, indeed, are interesting questions. The following aids are given to help establish a basic approach to understanding this fascinating work of inspired literature.

STYLES OF WRITING

Ecclesiastes is classified as wisdom literature. The Hebrew scripture is divided into three sections – Law, Writings and Prophets. The wisdom literature is located in the second division. At times, the third division absorbs the second division or Writings, leaving only the Law and Prophets. Writings would include the Old Testament books of Job, Psalms, Proverbs, Ecclesiastes and Song of Solomon. These books are somewhat different than other inspired books in style, form and purpose. The Hebrew wisdom literature parallels the wisdom literature of other ancient civilizations. The ancient Egyptians and the Babylonians had similar proverbs and thought-provoking material.

For example, *The Instruction of Amen-em-opet*, an ancient Egyptian text dated somewhere between the 10th and sixth centuries B.C., bears many parallels to Hebrew wisdom literature. Note the similar themes in it and Psalm 1:

> As for the heated man of a temple,
> He is like a tree growing in the open.
> In the completion of a moment (comes) its loss of foliage,
> And its end is reach in the shipyards;
> (Or) it is floated far from its place,

And the flame is its burial shroud.
(But) the truly silent man holds himself apart.
He is like a tree growing in a garden.
It flourishes and doubles its yield;
It (stands) before its lord.
Its fruit is sweet; its shade is pleasant;
And its end is reached in the garden. (*ANET* 422)

Another section has a striking resemblance to Proverbs 22:24:

Do not associate to thyself the heated man,
Nor visit him for conversation. (*ANET* 423)

One of the most interesting ancient texts is the Akkadian fable, *Ludlul Bel Nemeqi*, often referred to as the "Babylonian Job" because it addresses the theme of human suffering. As Job bemoaned his dire circumstances (Job 3:1-26), note the similar depth of despair:

My god has forsaken me and disappeared,
My goddess has cut me off and stayed removed from me.
The benevolent spirit who was (always) beside [me] has
    departed,
My protective spirit has flown away and seeks someone
    else.
My dignity has been taken away, my manly good looks
    jeopardized,
My pride has been cut off, my protection has skipped off.
Terrifying omens have been brought upon me,
I was put out of my house and wandered about outside.
    (*ANET* 596)

As the Lord restored Job's fortunes and health (Job 42:10-17), so also the "Babylonian Job" is blessed in a similar way by his god.

The Lord took hold of me,
The Lord set me on my feet,
The Lord restored me to health,
He rescued me [from the pit],
[…] he pulled me from the Hubur river,

[…] he took my hand.
[The one who] (once) struck me down,
Marduk (now) raised me up. (*ANET* 600)

Such connection between Hebrew wisdom and the wisdom of other ancient civilizations serves to demonstrate the universality of wisdom in general.

Every civilization has sought to provide material to instruct its citizens about proper behavior and attitudes. However, the wisdom material in the Old Testament is unique because God has certified by inspiration its content (2 Timothy 3:16). Thus, the wisdom contained in this literature instructs people how to live according to the will of God.

• *Reflective Wisdom.* Wisdom literature seeks to help us think about our lives, including the destiny toward which we are moving. Ecclesiastes, although instructive, is actually what may be called reflective wisdom. Reflective wisdom involves the relentless probing and questioning of traditional ideas and beliefs. Ecclesiastes employs this style to arouse thought and contemplation: "Consider the work of God, For who is able to straighten what He has bent? In the day of prosperity be happy, But in the day of adversity consider – God has made the one as well as the other So that man may not discover anything that will be after him" (Ecclesiastes 7:13-14).

The word "consider" in Ecclesiastes 7:14 is a call to reflect upon a profound spiritual matter. This is what wisdom literature seeks to achieve: if everyone thinks for themselves, they will not be so easily misled.

• *Shock.* Another style used in wisdom literature to arouse thought is to shock its readers with disturbing statements and observations. For example, notice how the book of Ecclesiastes begins: "'Vanity of vanities,' says the Preacher, 'Vanity of vanities! All is vanity'" (Ecclesiastes 1:2).

This statement is not a typical introduction for a book. It encourages the mind to contemplate what the Preacher means and why he would make such a declaration. This next example is even more shocking:

There is an evil which I have seen under the sun and it is prevalent among men – a man to whom God has given riches and wealth and honor so that his soul lacks nothing of all that he desires, but God has not empowered him to eat from them, for a foreigner enjoys them. This is vanity and a severe affliction. If a man fathers a hundred children and lives many years, however many they be, but his soul is not satisfied with good things, and he does not even have a proper burial, then I say, "Better the miscarriage than he, for it comes in futility and goes into obscurity; and its name is covered in obscurity. It never sees the sun and it never knows anything; it is better off than he. Even if the other man lives a thousand years twice and does not enjoy good things – do not all go to one place?" (Ecclesiastes 6:1-6)

A more pessimistic statement about life could not have been made. Is the Preacher to be taken seriously? Is this the way he really feels? One thing is certain – statements like these force us to consider what has just been said.

As with any book in the Bible, we must interpret scripture within its context. This is especially true with Ecclesiastes. It is easy to abuse if not kept in context. One example of abuse is found in one of its most notable texts:

There is an appointed time for everything. And there is a time for every event under heaven –

A time to give birth, and a time to die;
A time to plant, and a time to uproot what is planted.
A time to kill, and a time to heal;
A time to tear down, and a time to build up.
A time to weep, and a time to laugh;
A time to mourn, and a time to dance.
A time to throw stones, and a time to gather stones;
A time to embrace, and a time to shun embracing.
A time to search, and a time to give up as lost;
A time to keep, and a time to throw away.
A time to tear apart, and a time to sew together;
A time to be silent, and a time to speak.
A time to love, and a time to hate;
A time for war, and a time for peace. (Ecclesiastes 3:1-8)

We could reason from the above text a moral justification to kill, hate or even go to war; however, the Preacher is not attaching any moral or religious significance to the above-appointed times. He is merely recording his observations about life. In its context, time is also futile and cyclical. Humans are powerless to do anything about it. They are slaves of time and its seasons. This interpretation paints a completely different picture and is consistent with the vanity theme of the book.

• *Contrasting Themes*. Another style is the use of contrasting themes. These contrasts would include, but are not limited to, themes involving the wise and foolish, the righteous and wicked, the intelligent and simple, and of course, the rich and poor. The purpose of such contrasts is to define and illustrate proper behavior within God's universe. The irony in Ecclesiastes is that these contrasting themes confuse more than clarify. Although the Preacher commends wisdom over foolishness and righteousness over wickedness, no apparent reason appears to justify the pursuit of either wisdom or righteousness: "Do not be excessively righteous, and do not be overly wise. Why should you ruin yourself?" (Ecclesiastes 7:16). "So I said, 'Wisdom is better than strength.' But the wisdom of the poor man is despised and his words are not heeded. ... Wisdom is better than weapons of war, but one sinner destroys much good" (9:16, 18).

• *Proverbs*. Another style found in wisdom literature is arranging instructional material in the form of proverbs. In the book of Ecclesiastes, the most typical proverbial forms are the "better than" sayings. This form follows the pattern of stating that A is better than B. This method amplifies the preferred behavior or attitude God wants us to adopt. A collection of these proverbs is located in Ecclesiastes 7:1-8:

> A good name is better than a good ointment,
> And the day of one's death is better than the day of one's
>   birth.
> It is better to go to a house of mourning
> Than to go to a house of feasting,
> Because that is the end of every man,
> And the living takes it to heart.
> Sorrow is better than laughter,

For when a face is sad a heart may be happy.
The mind of the wise is in the house of mourning,
While the mind of fools is in the house of pleasure.
It is better to listen to the rebuke of a wise man
Than for one to listen to the song of fools.
For as the crackling of thorn bushes under a pot,
So is the laughter of the fool,
And this too is futility.
For oppression makes a wise man mad,
And a bribe corrupts the heart.
The end of a matter is better than its beginning;
Patience of spirit is better than haughtiness of spirit.

• *Rhetorical Questions.* In addition to the styles already mentioned, one final style appears to be the Preacher's favorite way of eliciting reader interaction. He employs rhetorical questions throughout Ecclesiastes. A rhetorical question requires no direct response but is designed to stimulate thought. The theme and the context of a rhetorical question determine the character of the thought. For example, the book opens with a question: "What advantage does man have in all his work Which he does under the sun?" (Ecclesiastes 1:3). The conclusion is, "No advantage." Thus the Preacher continually illustrates how misinformed and inept we are in our attempt to know how to conduct our lives. On several occasions, the Preacher asks, "Who knows?" (Ecclesiastes 2:19; 3:21; 6:12; 8:1). And the thoughtful response is naturally, "We certainly don't!"

Wisdom literature seeks to confirm our inability to make sense of life. One way Ecclesiastes establishes the necessity of having God's guidance is to reveal the limits of human wisdom. In Ecclesiastes, human wisdom is inadequate and incapable of understanding life fully (Ecclesiastes 7:23; 8:16-17).

So I turned to consider wisdom, madness and folly, for what will the man do who will come after the king except what has already been done? And I saw that wisdom excels folly as light excels darkness. The wise man's eyes are in his head, but the fool walks in darkness. And yet I know that one fate befalls them both. Then I said to myself, "As is the fate of the fool, it will also befall me. Why then have I been extremely wise?" So I said to myself, "This too is vanity." For there is no lasting remembrance of the wise man as with the fool, inasmuch as in the coming days all will be forgotten. And how the wise man and the fool alike die! So I hated life, for the work which had been done under the sun was grievous to me; because everything is futility and striving after wind. (Ecclesiastes 2:12-17)

The Preacher appears to mean that endeavoring to make sense out of life without God is an exercise in futility. The declarations that he hated life and that life was grievous to him are evidence of this.

The limitation of human wisdom is not only apparent in secular life but also in understanding religious truths. To demonstrate this flaw, the Preacher attacks what is customarily known as the theory of retribution, which is the common belief that good behavior is *always* rewarded and bad behavior is *always* punished. Although this theory sounds good, it is not true: "There is futility which is done on the earth, that is, there are righteous men to whom it happens according to the deeds of the wicked. On the other hand, there are evil men to whom it happens according to the deeds of the righteous. I say that this too is futility" (Ecclesiastes 8:14).

Job struggled with the same problem, as does Psalm 73. Life does not always reward the righteous and punish the wicked. Much of the time the exact opposite appears to be true. Once more, humans are incapable of providing any explanation.

As we read Ecclesiastes, it becomes clear that the Preacher seeks not to answer any of our questions. Every "Why?" is countered by "Who knows?" The Preacher has a subtle purpose to this blatant sidestep. He is moving us away from asking the question "Why?" and toward trusting in the "Who" – God!

THE AUTHOR

Ecclesiastes claims to be the words of the "Preacher," a term that refers to an office or occupation and not necessarily to any particular person. Regardless of the identity of the Preacher, the emphasis is placed upon the fact that the Preacher or Teacher is an instructor of wisdom. "The words of the Preacher, the son of David, king in Jerusalem" (Ecclesiastes 1:1).

At first, it is easy to concede Solomon is the author of Ecclesiastes. He seems to fit the description. He was endowed with great wisdom (1 Kings 4:29-34). That fact alone would qualify him as a great preacher and teacher. Solomon was also the son of David, serving as king over Israel for 40 years after his father's reign. In fact, Jewish rabbis finally acknowledged Ecclesiastes as part of the Hebrew canon because of the traditional view that Solomon wrote the book.

However, some difficulties arise with the view of Solomon as the author of Ecclesiastes. First, no scripture includes an indication that after Solomon departed from God he ever returned. Could Ecclesiastes be Solomon's epistle of repentance? This seems unlikely in view of the scriptural evidence:

> Now King Solomon loved many foreign women along with the daughter of Pharaoh: Moabite, Ammonite, Edomite, Sidonian, and Hittite women, from the nations concerning which the Lord had said to the sons of Israel, "You shall not associate with them, neither shall they associate with you, for they will surely turn your heart away after their gods." Solomon held fast to these in love. And he had seven hundred wives, princesses, and three hundred concubines, and his wives turned his heart away. ... and his heart was not wholly devoted to the Lord his God, as the heart of David his father had been. ... And Solomon did what was evil in the sight of the Lord, and did not follow the Lord fully, as David his father had done. ... Now the Lord was angry with Solomon because his heart was turned away from the Lord, the God of Israel, who had appeared to him twice, and had commanded him concerning this thing, that he should not go after other gods; but he did not observe what the Lord had commanded. So the Lord said to Solomon, "Because you have done this, and you have not

> kept My covenant and My statutes, which I have com-
> manded you, I will surely tear the kingdom from you, and
> will give it to your servant." (1 Kings 11:1-11)

Because Solomon departed from God, he would be an unfit witness to the aim of Ecclesiastes – to fear God and keep His commandments.

Second, the author of Ecclesiastes is not an apostate. Although some have asserted that he was, the purpose of Ecclesiastes – to lead us to faith in God – demonstrates the opposite (Ecclesiastes 12:13-14).

Third, the emphasis as to the credibility of the author is placed upon David. The mere fact that David is mentioned in the text entices people to read the book because of the profound reverence people have for one of Israel's most acclaimed leaders.

Finally, Solomon is never identified as the author by name, and the title mentioned in Ecclesiastes 1:1 is unspecific. Any son of David who may have reigned in Jerusalem could potentially be identified as the Preacher.

Ecclesiastes is best understood as a pseudonymous work; that is, a work where the author writes under a different name. The purpose of such a technique is to place the attention upon the message instead of the messenger. Ecclesiastes reads like an interactive biography in which Solomon is the perfect test-case to prove the author's point. Any reader could not help thinking of Solomon's failure at life while reading about the Preacher's materialistic, sexual and worldly pursuits. The very point the author wishes to make is that even the wisest human who ever lived is dependent upon God!

A JOURNEY OF FAITH

Ecclesiastes is about a journey. The journey is not shrouded in false illusions of grandeur. Nor is the journey discouraged. The unique feature about Ecclesiastes is its honest appraisal of what life is like without God and also with God. The latter is preferred because God is the Sovereign of the universe and the Judge of human destiny. God is the answer and solution to all human frustration and confusion. The only question remaining is whether you will trust God.

The conclusion of Ecclesiastes is much more profound than what appears on the surface: "The conclusion, when all has been heard, is:

fear God and keep His commandments, because this applies to every person. For God will bring every act to judgment, everything which is hidden, whether it is good or evil" (Ecclesiastes 12:13-14).

The journey in Ecclesiastes is really a journey of faith. This faith is not shallow or charismatic or without inward struggle. The author is preparing people who take the journey of faith for a difficult yet rewarding adventure. The journey will be difficult because we are required to hold God in the highest esteem even when life does not make sense. The journey of faith will also be demanding. Against human reason, we're required to keep the commandments of God. Without answers to some of the most fundamental questions about life, God's expectation of obedience can be taxing upon the human spirit. Again, trust (faith) is the key to success. Finally, the journey will require dedication. Every act will be brought into judgment. We will be derailed if we are not focused upon the road we are traveling. The word from the Preacher is not that the journey will be free from incident but that the destination will ultimately be reached.

QUESTIONS FOR PERSONAL AND GROUP REFLECTION

1. What is your opinion about the practical usefulness of Ecclesiastes in the life of a Christian? See Romans 15:4.

2. List and describe the different techniques the author of Ecclesiastes employs to grab the attention of his readers.

3. Who seems to be the author of Ecclesiastes? What evidence supports your conclusion?

4. What is the general purpose of wisdom literature? How does it differ in style and form from other types of biblical literature – narrative, prophecy, epistles, etc.? How is the wisdom literature in the Bible different from similar literature in other cultures?

5. Describe how Ecclesiastes presents the life of faith. Refer to Ecclesiastes 12:13-14.

2

SEEKING PURPOSE, FINDING FUTILITY

*Human life is everywhere a state in which much is
to be endured, and little to be enjoyed.*
– Samuel Johnson (1759)

*For what does a man get in all his labor and in his striving
with which he labors under the sun? Because all his days his
task is painful and grievous; even at night his mind does not
rest. This too is vanity. (Ecclesiastes 2:22-23)*

A little boy was in the habit of bringing a note from home when he
was late for class or had missed class altogether. His teacher had
asked the students to bring their birth certificates to class with them.
Because he had forgotten to bring his, the lad got up from his desk,
walked to the teacher and said, "Ma'am, I'm sorry, but I forgot my excuse for being born."

People – men or women, young or old, white collar or blue collar –
have periods in their lives when they feel compelled to search for their
purpose in life. Such a search usually commences during mid-life and
can be difficult for some people.

It is a time when the lively and colorful dreams and passions
of youth have given way to the mundane and the predictable.
It is the point at which the routine of life extinguishes the
romance of life. During this time relationships fail, religion
seems irrelevant, and the behavior of once sensible people
is baffling. From deep within the soul, one yearns for purpose. (Gleaves 13)

As the little schoolboy apologized for forgetting his "excuse for being born," other people are seeking their own excuse for being born.

We get up in the morning, go to work, come home, invest
in our family or friends, and go to bed – and we don't know

why. We don't know why we're working so hard, studying so hard, why we're married and trying to be committed to that marriage, or why we are working hard at being parents. We know why we're doing it on a superficial level – we work to make money, we study to make good grades, we stay married because we value commitment and it is often more practical to stay with one person over a long period of time, and we work hard at being parents because we love our children – but we don't know why we are living our life in an ultimate sense. It's tough to give, work, and sacrifice without knowing what it's all for in the end. (White 11)

Where can we find meaning in life? How can we sort through what is superficial and what is substantive about life? Is there really a higher or ultimate purpose to human existence? Ecclesiastes is addressed to those of us who have come to the point in our lives when we begin to ask, "Is this all there is?" The Preacher's message is for people lost in a dark tunnel, searching for a light at the end.

VANITY OF VANITIES

Would you be shocked to learn that Ecclesiastes appears to confirm the futility of life? The book opens by declaring life is vanity. But it is more than just vanity, as the superlative indicates – it is vanity of vanities. In other words, the situation is not just bad; it cannot get any worse.

The vanity theme is the key that unlocks Ecclesiastes. The Preacher uses the word "vanity" (Hebrew, *hebel*) more than 30 times, and the book itself forms what is referred to as an inclusion. The purpose of an inclusion is to establish the context in which a reader is to interpret the message. Any interpretation of the message of the book of Ecclesiastes must be consistent with its theme of vanity; otherwise, the text can be abused and distorted. This principle is true because the book begins and ends with the famous vanity statements: " 'Vanity of vanities,' says the Preacher, 'Vanity of vanities! All is vanity' " (Ecclesiastes 1:2). " 'Vanity of vanities,' says the Preacher, 'all is vanity!' " (12:8). These two passages form the inclusion and provide the interpretive key to the contents in between.

Because the vanity theme is central to Ecclesiastes, it is important to have a clear understanding of how the Preacher uses the term. The word "vanity" refers to how utterly useless, empty, meaningless and futile a person, object, thing, behavior or idea might be. Many parallel words or phrases convey the theme of vanity. Examples in Ecclesiastes would be: "striving after the wind," "nothing new under the sun," "no profit under the sun," "vanity under the sun," "grievous task," "grievous evil," "this too is futility," and "fleeting." Each of these words or phrases expresses the very character of vanity. Their use by the Preacher amplifies how vain life really is.

WHY IS LIFE MEANINGLESS?

Any reader would find the emphasis on the vanity of life disturbing. This was one of the major reasons Jewish rabbis had difficulty accepting Ecclesiastes into the Hebrew canon. Is the Preacher too pessimistic about life? Has he gone overboard and written a book of heresy? The confusion and the problems surrounding the interpretation of Ecclesiastes center on what the Preacher considers vain and in what sense this vanity is to be understood.

As many as 13 clear ideas are presented by the Preacher in Ecclesiastes carrying the infamous stamp of vanity.

1. *Everything about life is vanity.* This declaration has already been seen in Ecclesiastes 1:2 and 12:8. Nothing in life escapes its judgment. The inclusion is unmistakably broad in its application.

2. *All activity under the sun is vanity.* This statement is similar to the first one. The only difference appears to be the emphasis upon the futility of human activity – whatever is done. "Under the sun" is a reference to the world and its inhabitants. According to the Preacher, such vanity was enough to cause him to disdain life: "I have seen all the works which have been done under the sun, and behold, all is vanity and striving after wind" (Ecclesiastes 1:14). "So I hated life, for the work which had been done under the sun was grievous to me; because everything is futility and striving after wind" (2:17).

3. *Human joy is vanity.* The Preacher does not find enjoyment even in laughter or pleasure. As he relates in one passage, it is better to be in a house of mourning than to be at a feast (Ecclesiastes 7:2). In oth-

er words, attending a funeral for a joyful experience is far better than attending a wedding: "I said to myself, 'Come now, I will test you with pleasure. So enjoy yourself.' And behold, it too was futility. I said of laughter, 'It is madness,' and of pleasure, 'What does it accomplish?' " (2:1-2).

4. *Human wisdom is vanity.* Human intelligence has been unable to solve the problems of the world or answer the tough questions about faith. Because human intelligence and wisdom cannot offer an explanation about how life works, and in the end do not appear to differentiate between the one who has wisdom from the one who does not, it seems futile, therefore, to seek more human wisdom: "Then I said to myself, 'As is the fate of the fool, it will also befall me. Why then have I been extremely wise?' So I said to myself, 'This too is vanity' " (Ecclesiastes 2:15).

5. *Human industry is vanity.* Our human drive to better ourselves, provide a living, and enjoy the fruits of our labors is apparently a futile enterprise. The proverbial early bird who gets the worm finds no meaning in the book of Ecclesiastes. Human industry may have some advantages, but in the end, it robs the laborer of rest and satisfaction: "For what does a man get in all his labor and in his striving with which he labors under the sun? Because all his days his task is painful and grievous; even at night his mind does not rest. This too is vanity" (Ecclesiastes 2:22-23).

6. *Being a human being is vanity.* We could understand human pride leading to vanity, but to state emphatically that existing as a human being is also vanity is difficult to imagine. The Bible holds a high view of human beings. After all, people were created in the image of God. However, the Preacher challenges us with the sobering thought that we are not as special as we have imagined ourselves to be: "For the fate of the sons of men and the fate of beasts is the same. As one dies so dies the other; indeed, they all have the same breath and there is no advantage for man over beast, for all is vanity" (Ecclesiastes 3:19).

According to the Preacher, a human being has no advantage over the animal kingdom.

7. *The fruits of labor are vanity.* The Preacher denounces human industry by declaring the rewards of our work are not all that significant:

"And I have seen that every labor and every skill which is done is the result of rivalry between a man and his neighbor. This too is vanity and striving after wind" (Ecclesiastes 4:4).

This statement illustrates the enslaving adage of "keeping up with the Joneses." It is another way of saying a person cannot and will not win the rat race. The Preacher continues to show the vanity of how people are enslaved by greed.

> Then I looked again at vanity under the sun. There was a certain man without a dependent, having neither a son nor a brother, yet there was no end to all his labor. Indeed, his eyes were not satisfied with riches and he never asked, "And for whom am I laboring and depriving myself of pleasure?" This too is vanity and it is a grievous task. (Ecclesiastes 4:7-8)

Money cannot provide fulfillment in life or, in the pursuit of it, a joyful heart. Much of what the Preacher states about money and riches reminds us of similar statements Jesus made about seeking riches: "He who loves money will not be satisfied with money, nor he who loves abundance with its income. This too is vanity" (Ecclesiastes 5:10; Luke 12:15).

8. *Much dreaming and many words are vanity*. The Preacher does not place a premium on human vision and achievement. Dreams are but illusions, and to talk about them is to set ourselves up for a big disappointment. How many people truly live out their dreams anyway? "For in many dreams and in many words there is emptiness. Rather, fear God" (Ecclesiastes 5:7).

9. *The few days of life are vanity*. The Bible is replete with references about the brevity of life. Job bemoaned how man, "who is born of woman, Is short-lived and full of turmoil" (Job 14:1). The New Testament describes life as a "vapor that appears for a little while and then vanishes away" (James 4:14). The Preacher echoes the same sentiment: "For who knows what is good for a man during his lifetime, during the few years of his futile life? He will spend them like a shadow. For who can tell a man what will be after him under the sun?" (Ecclesiastes 6:12).

10. *The Preacher's life is vanity*. The Preacher holds out no hope for

his own life. While making observations about life, he admits how even his life is nothing but a lifetime of futility. A casual reader may wonder why anyone would bother reading his book: "I have seen everything during my lifetime of futility; there is a righteous man who perishes in his righteousness, and there is a wicked man who prolongs his life in his wickedness" (Ecclesiastes 7:15).

11. *The life of the reader is vanity.* Not only is the Preacher's life one of futility, but he also suggests your life is equally futile: "Enjoy life with the woman whom you love all the days of your fleeting life which He has given to you under the sun; for this is your reward in life, and in your toil in which you have labored under the sun" (Ecclesiastes 9:9).

The reader is assumed to be a married man, filled with ambition and hope for the future. Although he admits there might be some joy in life, it will surely pass so quickly as to make it nonexistent – a "fleeting [futile] life."

12. *The future is vanity.* Human beings typically are optimistic about the prospects of the future. The human spirit clings to hope. However, from the perspective of the Preacher, the future will be a huge disappointment. "Indeed, if a man should live many years, let him rejoice in them all, and let him remember the days of darkness, for they shall be many. Everything that is to come will be futility" (Ecclesiastes 11:8).

13. *Youthful vigor is vanity.* The American culture is a youth-oriented society. Youth is idolized, and old age is deemed an appendage and a drain upon society. Youth are the pride and joy of the future. The aged are the dregs remaining of the past. The Preacher sees it otherwise. Youth holds no promise; it is only a fleeting remembrance: "So, remove vexation from your heart and put away pain from your body, because childhood and the prime of life are fleeting" (Ecclesiastes 11:10).

WHY SO PESSIMISTIC?

We may wonder why the Preacher is so pessimistic about life. Had he failed miserably and become disillusioned with life in general? Could he have experienced a tragedy and that event colored his world with doom and gloom? Perhaps religion let him down, and now he had become the antagonist of traditional religious views. Just what is his problem?

The truth is the Preacher does not have a vendetta against life or any one person. His pessimism about life is an admission that a life without God is vain no matter how you may look at it. The lives of people who live without God's guidance and without trust in God are vain and striving after the wind. Life without God matters not! It is only an exercise in futility.

On the other hand, living a life in submission to God's will is a life with purpose and meaning. This is the Preacher's message in Ecclesiastes. The only life that counts is the life lived for God. Paul said the very same thing in the New Testament: "Therefore, my beloved brethren, be steadfast, immovable, always abounding in the work of the Lord, knowing that your toil is not in vain in the Lord" (1 Corinthians 15:58).

QUESTIONS FOR PERSONAL AND GROUP REFLECTION

1. Describe the Preacher's view of life. What methods does he employ to communicate his view?

2. Describe your reaction to the Preacher's belief that all of life is vanity.

3. Do you agree or disagree with the 13 vanity declarations? Why?

4. Describe the kind of audience you believe the Preacher is targeting with his vanity message.

5. How could you use the Preacher's message about the vanity of life in an evangelistic setting?

SEEKING FULFILLMENT, FINDING REGRET

What fools these mortals be.
– Seneca, Epistles, I, 3

Thus I hated all the fruit of my labor
for which I had labored under the sun,
for I must leave it to the man
who will come after me. (Ecclesiastes 2:18)

On a bookshelf flanking my desk is a plaque at eye level. I have angled it toward me so I will see it every day when I am in my study. The plaque has a picture of a monkey scratching his head with a pencil. The caption reads: "The more I study, the more I learn. The more I learn, the more I realize I don't know. So why study?"

A bit of wisdom is in this humorous statement. No matter how much we learn, we can never know it all!

When I turn to the bookshelf behind my desk, another point of interest is next to my telephone. Every time I reach for the receiver I see a framed counted cross-stitched picture my wife made for me. The picture shows a number of rats in running shoes dressed in Bermuda shorts competing in a race against each other. The words at the bottom of the picture say: "The rat race is over; the rats won!"

My wife knows my weakness very well. I'm the kind of guy who is always looking for his ship to appear. I can't count the number of money-making schemes I have tried in order to "make it big." I'm a sucker. I have sold vacuum cleaners, personal alarm systems and insurance. I have even traded stocks via the Internet. Unfortunately, I have risked and lost money in foolish enterprises, investment scams and business ventures. About every six to 12 months, I will get an itch to jump into the rat race again thinking I'll win big this time. But I won't because no one wins the rat race without suffering tremendous losses. The losses may include much more than just money. The loss could be health, family and peace of mind. The point is that no matter how much we may earn we can never earn enough to be satisfied.

The Preacher paints a dismal picture of life "under the sun," a phrase used exclusively in Ecclesiastes. This life to which the Preacher refers is the life one lives in complete disregard to God. We might designate it as a secular life – a life filled with unfulfilled dreams, aspirations and hopes. The secular life promises the joys of the world but delivers only pain, sorrow, frustration and disillusionment. The New Testament sums up the secular life this way:

> Do not love the world, nor the things in the world. If anyone loves the world, the love of the Father is not in him. For all that is in the world, the lust of the flesh and the lust of the eyes and the boastful pride of life, is not from the Father, but is from the world. And the world is passing away, and also its lusts; but the one who does the will of God abides forever. (1 John 2:15-17)

The lust of the flesh, lust of the eyes, and the pride of life remain the three most common delusions about secular life. The Preacher addresses these three seductive powers under two broad themes: wisdom and pleasure.

THE SEDUCTIVE POWER OF WISDOM

The most capable student of wisdom was Solomon. He was unmatched in his wisdom and in his ability and freedom to search out the meaning of life. His story is unique and worth reviewing: "In Gibeon the Lord appeared to Solomon in a dream at night; and God said, 'Ask what you wish me to give you' " (1 Kings 3:5).

God left the choice wide open for Solomon. Anything he wanted, he could ask God for. Solomon's request is surprising. One would perhaps think Solomon should have asked for fame and fortune. However, his request was most mature:

> O Lord my God, Thou hast made Thy servant king in place of my father David, yet I am but a little child; I do not know

how to go out or come in. And Thy servant is in the midst of Thy people which Thou hast chosen, a great people who cannot be numbered or counted for multitude. So give Thy servant an understanding heart to judge Thy people to discern between good and evil. For who is able to judge this great people of Thine?" (1 Kings 3:7-9)

Solomon realized how inadequate he was to achieve the task before him. He also knew how only God could provide what he lacked in the areas of leadership, justice and mercy. God was pleased with Solomon's spiritual discernment and promised to give him the things he did not ask for – namely, fame and fortune.

And it was pleasing in the sight of the Lord that Solomon had asked this thing. And God said to him, "Because you have asked this thing and have not asked for yourself long life, nor have asked riches for yourself, nor have you asked for the life of your enemies, but have asked for yourself discernment to understand justice, behold, I have done according to your words. Behold, I have given you a wise and discerning heart, so that there has been no one like you before you, nor shall one like you arise after you. And I have also given you what you have not asked, both riches and honor, so that there will not be any among the kings like you all your days. And if you walk in My ways, keeping My statutes and commandments, as your father David walked, then I will prolong your days." (1 Kings 3:10-14)

One of Solomon's most famous demonstrations of wisdom and judgment came early in his reign. The case involved a dispute between two prostitutes about a dead child. One prostitute had accidentally killed her own child, then attempted to switch her deceased son for the other woman's living son. Both women claimed to be the mother of the living child. Solomon was able to determine the child's mother by threatening to kill it: the baby's true mother was willing to give her child to the other woman to prevent its death. "When all Israel heard of the judgment which the king had handed down, they feared the king; for they saw that the wisdom of God was in him to administer justice" (1 Kings 3:16-28).

Not only was Solomon developing a reputation of unparalleled wisdom and judgment, but he was also a prolific writer of wisdom material and a keen observer of life in general. "And men came from all peoples to hear the wisdom of Solomon, from all the kings of the earth who had heard of his wisdom" (1 Kings 4:34).

The case has been clearly shown why the life of Solomon would be chosen by the Preacher to illustrate the folly of human wisdom. No one else would have been more capable of initiating a search for the true meaning of life. Anyone who may doubt the seriousness and dedication of Solomon's quest need only to read how the Preacher portrays his dedication: "I, the Preacher, have been king over Israel in Jerusalem. And I set my mind to seek and explore by wisdom concerning all that has been done under heaven" (Ecclesiastes 1:12-13).

The sincerity and earnestness of his search are made clear by the phrase, "I set my mind." The Preacher presents Solomon as having an unwavering commitment to the task. His search, however, would not be superficial. Solomon would "seek" life's meaning; that is, he would study the subject in depth. Additionally, Solomon would "explore" life. This word conveys the idea of studying a subject thoroughly and broadly. Therefore, what Solomon learned from his investigation can be trusted with a great degree of certainty.

The Preacher in Ecclesiastes presents three major truths about life discovered by Solomon. These truths are universal in their application and in agreement with the major theme of the book – "vanity of vanities! All is vanity!"

• *First, the problems of life are unavoidable.* We cannot run away from life's trials because God has given all people the task of facing life's problems. The Preacher shows how searching for meaning in life is a "grievous task which God has given to the sons of men to be afflicted with" (Ecclesiastes 1:13). Facing life is unavoidable. This truth hits hardest in a society that seeks to escape the problems of life through stimulants or depressants. Sooner or later, however, every individual must face the problems of life: "This is the burden which, by God's decree, every man bears: the problem of life is no optional hobby" (Eaton 62).

• *Second, the problems of life are frustrating.* Human wisdom fails to provide solutions and answers to life's problems. In fact, human wisdom only frustrates the quest for meaning in life. All we can do is throw up our hands and confess we don't know. The secular or human quest for meaning has failed; the seductive power of wisdom has only delivered frustration. As the Preacher says, "[A]ll is vanity and striving after wind" (Ecclesiastes 1:14).

• *Finally, the search for human wisdom leads to folly.* The Preacher learned the problems of life could not be solved by wisdom. Of course, the Preacher is attacking wisdom found under the sun; that is, human wisdom or knowledge.

> What is crooked cannot be straightened, and what is lacking cannot be counted. I said to myself, "Behold, I have magnified and increased wisdom more than all who were over Jerusalem before me; and my mind has observed a wealth of wisdom and knowledge." And I set my mind to know wisdom and to know madness and folly; I realized that this also is striving after wind. Because in much wisdom there is much grief, and increasing knowledge results in increasing pain. (Ecclesiastes 1:15-18)

As intelligent as we may be, many things remain outside the reach of our intelligence. The Preacher says some things are crooked and cannot be straightened. No matter how creative or industrious we may be, certain issues call for another kind of wisdom. This wisdom is the kind that comes from God.

In the New Testament, Paul wrote about the foolishness of the Christian message. The Jews thought the Christian message lacked drama. After all, their history was filled with spectacular events such as the parting of the Red Sea. Jesus would have attained instant credibility with them if He had done what Satan wanted him to do – jump from the pinnacle of the temple. On the other hand, the Greeks thought the Christian message was intellectually inferior when compared to their great orators. They delighted in speculations and eloquent demonstrations of oratory. To both Jews and Greeks, Paul wrote:

> For since in the wisdom of God the world through its wisdom did not come to know God, God was well-pleased through the foolishness of the message preached to save

those who believe. For indeed Jews ask for signs, and Greeks search for wisdom; but we preach Christ crucified, to Jews a stumbling block, and to Gentiles foolishness, but to those who are the called, both Jews and Greeks, Christ the power of God and the wisdom of God. Because the foolishness of God is wiser than men, and the weakness of God is stronger than men. (1 Corinthians 1:21-25)

What Paul stated is precisely the point the Preacher made. The world through its wisdom cannot and will not come to know God nor the true meaning of life.

THE SEDUCTIVE POWER OF PLEASURE

Another seductive power of the world under the sun is the promise of fleshly pleasures. The Preacher immediately declares the verdict against pleasure:

I said to myself "Come now, I will test you with pleasure. So enjoy yourself." And behold, it too was futility. I said of laughter, "It is madness," and of pleasure, "What does it accomplish?" I explored with my mind how to stimulate my body with wine while my mind was guiding me wisely, and how to take hold of folly, until I could see what good there is for the sons of men to do under heaven the few years of their lives. (Ecclesiastes 2:1-3)

Frivolity leaves one with a definite emptiness. Laughter mixed with wine produces only momentary times of pleasure. Moral frivolity cannot serve as a guide to life or as a foundation to build a life upon. What does frivolity actually accomplish?

The Preacher demonstrates the emptiness of fame and fortune (Ecclesiastes 2:4-10). Again, Solomon is the perfect example. His fame and fortune were without equal in the ancient world. The Queen of Sheba heard so much concerning Solomon's wisdom that she traveled to Jerusalem specifically to test his abilities. She was not disappointed. He became the greatest king in the world, and people came to Jerusalem with gifts for him and to hear his wisdom (1 Kings 10:1-7, 23-25).

Despite Solomon's great fame and fortune, the Preacher declares that such secular possessions will leave us only empty inside: "Thus I considered all my activities which my hands had done and the labor which I had exerted, and behold all was vanity and striving after wind and there was no profit under the sun" (Ecclesiastes 2:11).

Perhaps the best way to understand the emptiness of pleasure is to think of it in terms of a drunkard. The Preacher shows how one finally had to face the morning after a drinking binge – the head pounds, and the stomach is queasy. Did Solomon have any regrets? Yes, he certainly did. "I considered" means "I faced." In other words, he owned up to the facts of his behavior the night before. Did he enjoy himself? He surely did. That is the real attraction. The hurt comes after the sin. For a fleeting moment nothing matters, and everything feels so good. The Hebrews writer in the New Testament refers to the "passing pleasures of sin" (Hebrews 11:25). Was this drinker satisfied with the experience? He certainly was not. He became completely disillusioned about life. Does the cycle repeat itself? Of course! That is how a life without God unfolds. Unfortunately, the emptiness compounds with each secular pursuit of pleasure.

A life without God does not need a moral judgment made against it to declare its utter folly; the godless life fails upon its own premises. Jesus faced the seduction of this world during a grueling 40-day period of temptations. Jesus countered and overcame the lure of the flesh, fame and fortune because of His relationship with God.

> It is written, "Man shall not live on bread alone, but on every word that proceeds out of the mouth of God."... On the other hand, it is written, "You shall not put the Lord your God to the test." ... Begone, Satan! For it is written, "You shall worship the Lord your God, and serve Him only." (Matthew 4:4, 7, 10)

God's wisdom and our relationship with Him are the only means of countering the seductive powers of the secular world.

QUESTIONS FOR PERSONAL AND GROUP REFLECTION

1. Why are people attracted to pleasure to the point of disregarding the pain that may follow?

2. In what ways is Solomon a credible test-case for evaluating the emptiness of worldly pursuits? Can you think of any reasons why he would not be a credible witness?

3. How does secular society perpetuate the human wisdom and pleasure deceptions?

4. What specific actions can Christians take to help themselves withstand the pressures and allurements of secular society?

5. In John 17, Jesus said in His prayer of unity that His disciples were in the world but not of the world. What did He mean by this, and how can Christians specifically apply His words to their lives?

4

SEEKING LIFE, FINDING DEATH

The fear of death is more to be dreaded than death itself.
– Publilius Syrus, Maxim 511 (1st Century B.C.)

The wise man's eyes are in his head,
but the fool walks in darkness.
And yet I know that one fate befalls
them both. (Ecclesiastes 2:14)

Jesus told a story about how a father's younger son once made a terrible choice. After receiving his inheritance, the younger son went to a distant country and wasted everything he had. He finally ended up eating food fit only for pigs. When the son decided to return home, he received a royal welcome from his father. The father viewed his son's return as if he had come back to life: "for this son of mine was dead, and has come to life again; he was lost, and has been found … for this brother of yours was dead and has begun to live, and was lost and has been found" (Luke 15:24, 32).

In his letter to the Ephesians, Paul described people living apart from God as dead although they had a biological existence: "And you were dead in your trespasses and sins, in which you formerly walked according to the course of this world, according to the prince of the power of the air, of the spirit that is now working in the sons of disobedience" (Ephesians 2:1-2).

In Ecclesiastes, death seems to be preferred over life. This is true because the book takes the position that life apart from God has no purpose or meaning. People attempting to go through life without God are in truth the living dead. To amplify how purposeless a godless life is, the Preacher spares no punches. However, the Preacher does not leave the godless without hope.

IS THERE HOPE WITHOUT GOD?

Hope plays a vital role in human motivation and productivity. If hope is lost, despair takes over. Before the Preacher provides any practical recommendations for overcoming despair, he destroys any false notions of hope the godless might have.

• *The memory of the godless will be forgotten.* Human beings in general have a strong desire to make a difference in the world. They want to make a name for themselves so that people might remember them long after they are gone. The Preacher attacks this fundamental desire in the very beginning of Ecclesiastes. "There is no remembrance of earlier things; And also of the later things which will occur, There will be for them no remembrance Among those who will come later still" (Ecclesiastes 1:11).

Nothing the godless can do or achieve guarantees them a lasting memory of all their efforts done under the sun. "For there is no lasting remembrance of the wise man as with the fool, inasmuch as in the coming days all will be forgotten. And how the wise man and the fool alike die!" (Ecclesiastes 2:16). All human achievement, human wisdom and human hope are completely erased by death. Even those who have distinguished themselves from fools suffer the same fateful end.

• *The legacy of the godless will be lost.* Human beings have a desire to leave something behind. Often Americans are reminded that their legacy is freedom. Parents want to provide a better future for their children. But every attempt to secure a better tomorrow or to provide a positive path for the next generation is vanity. This is true because the living cannot control the future. Who knows whether the next generation will be grateful or ungrateful? This very prospect, the Preacher suggests, caused the most grief:

> Thus I hated all the fruit of my labor for which I had labored under the sun, for I must leave it to the man who will come after me. And who knows whether he will be a wise man or a fool? Yet he will have control over all the fruit of my labor for which I have labored by acting wisely under the sun. This too is vanity. Therefore I completely despaired of all the fruit of my labor for which I had labored under the sun.

> When there is a man who has labored with wisdom, knowl-
> edge and skill, then he gives his legacy to one who has not
> labored with them. This too is vanity and a great evil. For
> what does a man get in all his labor and in his striving with
> which he labors under the sun? Because all his days his task
> is painful and grievous; even at night his mind does not rest.
> This too is vanity. (Ecclesiastes 2:18-23)

The Preacher admits the burden of the unknown is too much to bear.
A man may work his fingers to the bone to leave a legacy only to have
the fruits of his labor later squandered by a fool. Notice the strong language in the text: "I hated life" (Ecclesiastes 2:17), and "I completely despaired" (v. 20). The pain and the grief and the many restless nights
were at best a "great evil" (v. 21).

• *The pride of the godless will be humbled.* From a biblical perspective,
we would defend the distinctiveness of humans over animals. God created humans in His image and charged them with the task of oversee-
ing the earth. Humans, therefore, were God's climactic creation.
However, the Preacher asserts there is no real difference in value between animals and humans. The Preacher's perspective is unique. What
he says is true when understood that humans were created to have a relationship with God. This makes the human distinctive from all animals. When people turn away from God, they forfeit that part that makes
them unique and special. This perspective provides the interpretive
framework for the following verses:

> I said to myself concerning the sons of men, "God has sure-
> ly tested them in order for them to see that they are but
> beasts." For the fate of the sons of men and the fate of beasts
> is the same. As one dies so dies the other; indeed, they all
> have the same breath and there is no advantage for man over
> beast, for all is vanity. All go to the same place. All came
> from the dust and all return to the dust. Who knows that the
> breath of man ascends upward and the breath of the beast
> descends downward to the earth? (Ecclesiastes 3:18-21)

The test of God is a demonstration of how people without God are
mere animals. The essential element – God – who raises people above

the animal has been rejected. Consequently, a godless person's death is no more significant than the death of an animal. As one theologian suggested, "Man, by himself, becomes a 'naked ape'" (Eaton 85).

• *The hope of the godless will be their horror.* Finally, the Preacher offers a bit of hope to the godless. He suggests one advantage a living person has over a dead person – knowledge. Then the Preacher hammers the final nail into the coffin. The knowledge the living person has over the dead person is the knowledge that he is going to die.

> For whoever is joined with all the living, there is hope; surely a live dog is better than a dead lion. For the living know they will die; but the dead do not know anything, nor have they any longer a reward, for their memory is forgotten. Indeed their love, their hate, and their zeal have already perished, and they will no longer have a share in all that is done under the sun. (Ecclesiastes 9:4-6)

Surely it is better to be alive than dead; yet, the living are preoccupied and terrified by death. The writer of Hebrews talked about the fear of death:

> Since then the children share in flesh and blood, He Himself likewise also partook of the same, that through death He might render powerless him who had the power of death, that is, the devil; and might deliver those who through fear of death were subject to slavery all their lives. (Hebrews 2:14-15)

Death is not so terrifying to the person who walks with God.

DOES LIFE HAVE MEANING WITHOUT GOD?

After stripping the godless of any hope outside a relationship with God, the Preacher next reveals how meaningless life is without God. He demonstrates the meaninglessness of life under three powerful figures.

• *A life without God has as much meaning as one who is dead.* The Preacher views death as the cessation of all useful and constructive activity and memory. Although a person might be alive, if God is not in his life, he might as well be dead, for his life serves no purpose at all.

"So I congratulated the dead who are already dead more than the living who are still living" (Ecclesiastes 4:2). Why should the dead be congratulated? Does a person living without God have hope? Consider the example in the above text. To whom can the oppressed call out? What are the chances their cries for help will be heard? This text is the antithesis of the example of two Christian men, Paul and Silas. They called upon God for deliverance, and God heard them (Acts 16:22-30).

• *A life without God has as much meaning as one who has never been born.* The godless life serves no significant purpose in the world, nor provides any worthwhile help to others. Surely humans have made great contributions and tremendous strides to fight diseases, hunger and poverty. But the Preacher would ask, "To what end?" There is also much the human race continues to promote – violence, materialism and selfishness, to name only a few. "But better off than both of them is the one who has never existed, who has never seen the evil activity that is done under the sun" (Ecclesiastes 4:3).

• *A life without God has as much meaning as one who has been aborted.* This figure could be offensive to some who may misunderstand what the Preacher is saying. If what makes human life valuable is taken away, then human life ceases to be of value. Better to stop the process of maturation than to allow another human being to live a meaningless life under the sun.

> There is an evil which I have seen under the sun and it is prevalent among men – a man to whom God has given riches and wealth and honor so that his soul lacks nothing of all that he desires, but God has not empowered him to eat from them, for a foreigner enjoys them. This is vanity and a severe affliction. If a man fathers a hundred children and lives many years, however many they be, but his soul is not satisfied with good things, and he does not even have a proper burial, then I say, "Better the miscarriage than he, for it comes in futility and goes into obscurity; and its name is covered in obscurity. It never sees the sun and it never knows anything; it is better off than he. Even if the other man lives a thousand years twice and does not enjoy good things – do not all go to one place?" (Ecclesiastes 6:1-6)

FINDING PURPOSE IN LIFE

Contrary to the false hope of the godless life stands the religious conviction of the Preacher. God enters into the discussion in the early stages of His inspired book. In Ecclesiastes, the theme of fearing God offers true hope that people can find a purpose for their lives. This fear of God provides the foundation for a happy, fulfilled and truly meaningful life. Five keys to finding purpose for our lives are found in Ecclesiastes.

• *The first key to purposeful living is to stand before God in reverence.* "I know that everything God does will remain forever; there is nothing to add to it and there is nothing to take from it, for God has so worked that men should fear Him" (Ecclesiastes 3:14).

The word "fear" does not mean we should be afraid of or dread God. Fear means reverence – to stand before God in awe. This text reveals the missing element causing the emptiness of human life. The central factor to all meaningful life is acknowledging the sovereignty of God. People who deny God's sovereignty discard the very nature of their being and deny their only true source of happiness.

• *The second key to purposeful living is to hold God as top priority.* The first four commandments of the Ten Commandments affirm God's priority in the life of Israel – no other gods before Him; no graven images; do not take God's name in vain; remember the Sabbath to keep it holy. After the first four laws, the remaining six commandments address the relationship people are to have with one another. In other words, we must first be right with God before any relationship can be right with our fellow human beings.

Jesus once reminded His followers about the same thing: "But seek first His kingdom and His righteousness; and all these things shall be added to you" (Matthew 6:33). "These things" refers to the needs humans have, such as food, shelter and clothing. Despite those needs, the ultimate need of every human is to have God as his or her priority. "For in many dreams and in many words there is emptiness. Rather, fear God" (Ecclesiastes 5:7).

Human activity and planning are secondary to the human need for God. He is the One who provides meaning to dreams and aspirations.

• *The third key to purposeful living is to walk according to God's way.* In Proverbs, people are warned about trusting in themselves about

G. SCOTT GLEAVES • 45

how to live the right way: "There is a way which seems right to a man, But its end is the way of death" (Proverbs 14:12).

The Preacher states the matter in a somewhat different way.

> Do not be excessively righteous, and do not be overly wise. Why should you ruin yourself? Do not be excessively wicked, and do not be a fool. Why should you die before your time? It is good that you grasp one thing, and also not let go of the other; for the one who fears God comes forth with both of them. (Ecclesiastes 7:16-18)

The Preacher is not recommending moderation but is discouraging self-righteousness. The reader must keep in mind this perspective is the view from "under the sun." True righteousness is connected to God. The admonition to "not be overly wise" means not to play the part of a wise man. Neither is the Preacher encouraging moderation in evil. What is admitted is the godly walk between two extremes – shunning self-righteousness and avoiding evil behavior. This path leads to the attainment of true righteousness and true wisdom only the godly can possess.

• *The fourth key to purposeful living is to trust in God.* "Although a sinner does evil a hundred times and may lengthen his life, still I know that it will be well for those who fear God, who fear Him openly. But it will not be well for the evil man and he will not lengthen his days like a shadow, because he does not fear God" (Ecclesiastes 8:12-13).

A paradox surrounds the days of an evil man. Although the evil man may lengthen his days, in the final analysis his days are shortened. A change occurs in the language of the Preacher. Much of the material has been presented as something observed by everyone "under the sun." However, when the Preacher states "I know," he puts this knowledge in the realm of faith. For all practical purposes, living under the sun appears to fare better than godliness. The godly know, however, the true story – "it will not be well for the evil man."

• *The fifth key to purposeful living is to obey God.* Obedience to God is connected to a proper recognition of His authority and power. At the conclusion of Ecclesiastes, we'll face the crux of the matter. The choice must be made, and the matter cannot be avoided. Further persuasion or evidence is not needed. To this end, Ecclesiastes has been leading us: "The conclusion, when all has been heard, is: fear God and keep His commandments, because this applies to every person" (Ecclesiastes 12:13).

God has the power to give us life – a real, purposeful and meaningful life. The message of Ecclesiastes and Ephesians is that God can make the "dead" live again: "But God, being rich in mercy, because of His great love with which He loved us, even when we were dead in our transgressions, made us alive together with Christ (by grace you have been saved), and raised us up with Him, and seated us with Him in the heavenly places, in Christ Jesus" (Ephesians 2:4-6).

QUESTIONS FOR PERSONAL AND GROUP REFLECTION

1. How important is it for people to have hope? Describe how the Preacher differentiates between true hope and false hope. How is the Preacher's view of hope consistent with the teachings of the New Testament?

2. Do you feel compelled to leave your mark upon the world? Describe the kind of legacy you want to leave. How would the Preacher evaluate your legacy – permanent or temporary? Why?

3. According to the Preacher, what quality distinguishes humans from animals? List at least five ways this essential element can be developed and maintained.

4. Why do people fear death? What is the horror of death according to the Preacher? How does your relationship with God help you overcome the fear of death?

5. Discuss three ways the Preacher describes how meaningless life is without God. How does his discussion make you feel? Was he effective in his presentation? Explain.

5

SEEKING SUCCESS, FINDING FAILURE

And my ending is despair. – *Shakespeare,*
The Tempest, *Epilogue, l. 15*

*What profit is there to the worker from that in which
he toils? (Ecclesiastes 3:9)*

M oney will solve all your problems, right? We need money; we
work for it; we desire it. The Preacher says that most people
view money as the key to happiness. The world's motto would be: "Men
prepare a meal for enjoyment, and wine makes life merry, and money
is the answer to everything" (Ecclesiastes 10:19).

Work is the means to achieve the goal of success. Working hard is
the way to financial stability and success, right? One day our ship will
come in and everything will be perfect. Think again. Jesus said that
materialistic pursuits do not satisfy the real needs of people. "And He
said to them, 'Beware, and be on your guard against every form of
greed; for not even when one has an abundance does his life consist of
his possessions'" (Luke 12:15).

Greed is a powerful human emotion. Greed can come in many forms
– gambling, selfishness and envy, among others. The quest for material acquisitions has led many people to the divorce courts, bars and
drug alleys of America. Paul linked greed to idolatry (Colossians 3:5).
If an idol is an object to be worshiped, idolatry is the practice of idol
worship. Consequently, money and material possessions can indeed
become the objects of human worship.

THE EMPTINESS OF MATERIALISTIC AMBITIONS

The Preacher strips away all the hype surrounding the material world, exposing instead the wasteland of emptiness it really is. Toward what end does the working materialist invest his time and energy? The Preacher keeps reminding his readers: "What advantage does man have in all his work Which he does under the sun?" (Ecclesiastes 1:3; 2:11; 3:9; 5:16).

The question is valid. Does human toil provide what you really need? The Preacher does not believe the world "under the sun" offers all that much. He suggests the following reasons for our consideration:

• *The working materialist is caught in a meaningless cycle.* The opening poem in the book of Ecclesiastes explores the cycle of futility of human toil:

> A generation goes and a generation comes,
>> But the earth remains forever.
>
> Also, the sun rises and the sun sets;
>> And hastening to its place it rises there again.
>
> Blowing toward the south,
>> Then turning toward the north,
>
> The wind continues swirling along;
>> And on its circular courses the wind returns.
>
> All the rivers flow into the sea,
>> Yet the sea is not full.
>
> To the place where the rivers flow,
>> There they flow again.
>
> All things are wearisome;
>> Man is not able to tell it.
>
> The eye is not satisfied with seeing,
>> Nor is the ear filled with hearing.
>
> That which has been is that which will be,
>> And that which has been done is that which will be done.
>
> So, there is nothing new under the sun.
>> Is there anything of which one might say, "See this, it is new"?

Already it has existed for ages
    Which were before us.
There is no remembrance of earlier things;
    And also of the later things which will occur,
There will be for them no remembrance
    Among those who will come later still.
    (Ecclesiastes 1:4-11)

Human labor is compared to the endless movements of the sun, the sea and the wind. Their destinations are not apparent although each of them continues tirelessly. The sun rises and sets and then repeats the process. What exactly is the sun's destination? The rivers flow into the sea, the water evaporates, rains fall and fill the rivers, and the process repeats. Toward what end is the sea moving? The wind sets out on its circular rotation and then returns from where it began. Again, where is the wind's final destination? No wonder the Preacher speaks of this fruitless toil as "wearisome." Next, the Preacher makes the application to human industry. Human labor is ultimately as fruitless as the motions of the sun, sea and wind.

• *The working materialist is not appreciated.* His dedication, his well-conceived plans, and his many sleepless nights go unnoticed. The benefactors of his efforts squander the fruit of his labor. The Preacher asks why then do we exert so much effort?

Thus I hated all the fruit of my labor for which I had labored under the sun, for I must leave it to the man who will come after me. And who knows whether he will be a wise man or a fool? Yet he will have control over all the fruit of my labor for which I have labored by acting wisely under the sun. This too is vanity. Therefore I completely despaired of all the fruit of my labor for which I had labored under the sun. When there is a man who has labored with wisdom, knowledge and skill, then he gives his legacy to one who has not labored with them. This too is vanity and a great evil. For what does a man get in all his labor and in his striving with which he labors under the sun? Because all his days his task is painful and grievous; even at night his mind does not rest. This too is vanity. (Ecclesiastes 2:18-23)

• *The working materialist is motivated by envy.* The Preacher affirms the truth of the common cliché about "keeping up with the Joneses." The desire to have the advantage over one's neighbor seems unending.

> And I have seen that every labor and every skill which is done is the result of rivalry between a man and his neighbor. This too is vanity and striving after wind. The fool folds his hands and consumes his own flesh. One hand full of rest is better than two fists full of labor and striving after wind. (Ecclesiastes 4:4-6)

Henri Nouwen once gave a series of lectures on the spiritual aspects of a minister's work. These lectures were collected and printed in book form titled *The Way of the Heart*. Nouwen tells how ministers (and people in general) have been indoctrinated by life from the perspective of the general culture. He wrote:

> There is seldom a period in which we do not know what to do, and we move through life in such a distracted way that we do not even take the time and rest to wonder if any of the things we think, say, or do are *worth* thinking, saying, or doing. (Nouwen 21-22)

According to Nouwen, secular society has influenced the people of God more than they might be willing to admit. He describes life without God (secular society) as a "dangerous network of domination and manipulation in which we can easily get entangled and lose our soul." He wonders whether ministers have become blind to their own final state and that of people in general (21).

Why does Nouwen make such accusations against ministers primarily and the people of God generally? He bases his conclusions upon what he observes in the lives of God's people. He believes many people of faith live their lives within the fabric of secular life. They move in the direction that secularity chooses. For instance, if culture believes that money is the most important possession, then in response, people burden themselves with more and more work – even at the expense of family and health – in order to obtain it simply because this is what secular life values. Tragically, according to Nouwen, the cost of such living is too high. The two primary results of such compulsion, in his view, are anger and greed. These represent the two most deadly enemies of the spiritual life (23).

• *The working materialist is never satisfied.* Once a specific destination has been achieved, another one is quickly planned. A feeling of achievement cannot be permanently enjoyed because there is always a higher peak to climb. Life to the working materialist is a necessary evil until the object craved is obtained. Consequently, joy and happiness are connected to the end or destination. We'll never be happy, therefore, because the end is beyond our grasp.

> He who loves money will not be satisfied with money, nor he who loves abundance with its income. This too is vanity. When good things increase, those who consume them increase. So what is the advantage to their owners except to look on? The sleep of the working man is pleasant, whether he eats little or much. But the full stomach of the rich man does not allow him to sleep. ... All a man's labor is for his mouth and yet the appetite is not satisfied. (Ecclesiastes 5:10-12; 6:7)

The rich man cannot enjoy his rest because he is forever looking into the future, visualizing and planning his next material acquisition.

• *The working materialist cannot predict the future.* As hard as we might try to secure a fortune, we cannot control what the future may hold.

> There is a grievous evil which I have seen under the sun: riches being hoarded by their owner to his hurt. When those riches were lost through a bad investment and he had fathered a son, then there was nothing to support him. As he had come naked from his mother's womb, so will he return as he came. He will take nothing from the fruit of his labor that he can carry in his hand. And this also is a grievous evil – exactly as a man is born, thus will he die. So, what is the advantage to him who toils for the wind? Throughout his life he also eats in darkness with great vexation, sickness and anger. (Ecclesiastes 5:13-17)

Jesus illustrated this point when two brothers were arguing over an inheritance. When one brother tried to bring Jesus into the dispute, Jesus cautioned him about the dangers of the material. What we may think matters most, in the grand scheme of things, matters very little.

> And He told them a parable, saying, "The land of a certain rich man was very productive. And he began reasoning to himself, saying, 'What shall I do, since I have no place to store my crops?' And he said, 'This is what I will do: I will tear down my barns and build larger ones, and there I will store all my grain and my goods. And I will say to my soul, "Soul, you have many goods laid up for many years to come; take your ease, eat, drink and be merry.'" But God said to him 'You fool! This very night your soul is required of you; and now who will own what you have prepared?' So is the man who lays up treasure for himself, and is not rich toward God." (Luke 12:16-21)

HOW TO MAKE A LIFE WHILE EARNING A LIVING

The Preacher has exposed the emptiness of materialism. Obviously, there must be another way of viewing work and the kind of life that would bring satisfaction and joy. Within the message of Ecclesiastes are clues to a joyful life. One such clue comes early in the book. After the Preacher admits life under the sun offers no real hope or satisfaction, he makes this assertion: "There is nothing better for a man than to eat and drink and tell himself that his labor is good. This also I have seen, that it is from the hand of God. For who can eat and who can have enjoyment without Him?" (Ecclesiastes 2:24-25).

These optimistic statements are compelling in view of the fact that the Preacher has just stated that he hated life (Ecclesiastes 2:17), he despaired of the fruit of his labor (v. 20), and life was grievous to him (v. 23). Yet, from a totally different angle, he holds out a promise of a fulfilling life to us.

Three crucial elements are involved in a joyful life. The absence of any one of these three elements ruins the possibility of a purposeful existence.

• *The first crucial element of a joyful life is the foundation: Have faith in God.* True prosperity is linked to God and means more than money. The answer to the question, "Who can have enjoyment without Him?" (Ecclesiastes 2:25) is obvious. We cannot truly enjoy life – neither the journey nor the destination – without a meaningful relationship with the Creator. The goodness of life comes from the hand of God.

• *The second crucial element of a joyful life is contentment.* The phrase "eat and drink" in Ecclesiastes 2:24 is a Hebrew expression denoting contentment. Some people seem to have a distorted view of the biblical teaching of contentment. Does contentment mean settling for less? This cannot be the meaning of the term because the Preacher encourages his audience to excel in their endeavors (Ecclesiastes 9:10). Does not contentment imply failure? Not so; biblical contentment is connected to success. What then does the term "contentment" really mean? First Timothy 6:6-10 sheds light on the term:

> But godliness actually is a means of great gain, when accompanied by contentment. For we have brought nothing into the world, so we cannot take anything out of it either. And if we have food and covering, with these we shall be content. But those who want to get rich fall into temptation and a snare and many foolish and harmful desires which plunge men into ruin and destruction. For the love of money is a root of all sorts of evil, and some by longing for it have wandered away from the faith, and pierced themselves with many a pang.

Contentment allows us to enjoy the present regardless of what the future may or may not hold. Contentment is the key to happiness and the enjoyment of life simply because it does not depend on external circumstances.

• *The third crucial element of a joyful life is the journey.* An attitude of contentment brings about a new focus upon the present. The Preacher emphasizes the journey of life under the theme "fear God." Enjoying the journey is also a part of reaching the destination. The phrase "tell himself" (Ecclesiastes 2:24) implies that people need to remind themselves to enjoy the journey. Therefore, we can find pleasure and satisfaction in the present. "Sow your seed in the morning, and do not be idle in the evening, for you do not know whether morning or evening sowing will succeed, or whether both of them alike will be good" (Ecclesiastes 11:6).

Because God controls the future, people who fear Him confidently enjoy life and continue to be active in their labors. What the future holds is inconsequential.

Being good in God's sight and embracing the three crucial elements to a joyful life opens us up to even more blessings. The Preacher explains that God also bestows three gifts upon His children.

> For to a person who is good in His sight He has given wisdom and knowledge and joy, while to the sinner He has given the task of gathering and collecting so that he may give to one who is good in God's sight. This too is vanity and striving after wind. (Ecclesiastes 2:26)

• *The first gift from God is wisdom* (Ecclesiastes 2:14, 21; 7:12, 23; 8:1; 9:15, 18; 10:10). Proverbs, also part of the wisdom literature of the Old Testament, indicates the beginning of wisdom as the fear of the Lord (Proverbs 1:1-7; 4:5, 7). This is a consistent theme not only in Ecclesiastes and Proverbs but also in all of the wisdom literature (Job 28:28; Psalm 111:10). People living in harmony with God's will have a unique perspective of life. They see life through the lens of God's purpose and will. The folly of life "under the sun" does not fool them. Wisdom is discernment. And the ability to discern between good and evil, wisdom and folly, and joy and despair develops as our relationship with God matures.

• *The second gift from God is knowledge.* Knowledge refers more to learning from our experiences in life than to the accumulation of facts. The ability to learn from the positive and negative experiences of our lives as well as from the lives of others is a blessing from God. The testimony of Ecclesiastes is based upon what the Preacher has learned from his experiences. The knowledge he has gained is presented to us as lessons for life (Ecclesiastes 2:1-11). The events of Old Testament history are simply the inspired religious teachings of God's people, including negative and positive experiences. Each type provides knowledge.

• *The third gift from God is joy.* Joy is the ability to exult in God no matter what the circumstances. Joy, like all blessings, is directly linked to God. The phrase "eat, drink and be merry" throughout Ecclesiastes is a presentation of joyful living under the hand of God as opposed to the life of vanity under the sun (Ecclesiastes 3:12, 22; 5:18-20). Evidence of this kind of joy is seen in many of God's people, including (but not limited to) David, Daniel, Jesus and Paul.

David was able to exult in God although his son Absalom sought to destroy Him (Psalm 3). Daniel stood firm and exalted God when his enemies threw him into a lion's den (Daniel 6). Jesus exulted in God when He entrusted Himself to God at the crucifixion (Hebrews 12:1-2). Paul, along with Silas, sang songs of praises to God from the confines of a prison cell. All of these examples illustrate how the joy God gives us is not dependent upon anything found in this world, and nothing under the sun can take joy from us. An "under the sun" life leads to despair; the "good" life leads to delight!

QUESTIONS FOR PERSONAL AND GROUP REFLECTION

1. In what ways does secular culture encourage materialism? How should a person of faith respond to these allurements?

2. How does the Preacher's discussion about the working materialist affect you? In what ways do you agree or disagree with his evaluation? What point do you consider to be his best?

3. How does secular culture stimulate the vices of anger and greed? In what ways do secular standards of success demoralize faith and virtue?

4. Why is the virtue of contentment so difficult to attain? How can contentment protect you spiritually? Are there ways in which the church encourages materialism? How can the church help members to be content?

5. How can God's gifts according to Ecclesiastes equip you in your journey of faith? Why is it important to think of life as a journey instead of a destination?

6

SEEKING CONTROL, FINDING CHAOS

*Ninety-nine percent of the people in the world are fools
and the rest of us are in great danger of contagion.*
– Thornton Wilder, The Matchmaker, Act I *(1954)*

*I tested all this with wisdom, and I said, "I will be wise,"
but it was far from me. (Ecclesiastes 7:23)*

N o matter how we view it, some things in life just don't make sense.
We do not live in a nice, tidy world where everything fits together
like a jigsaw puzzle. Ecclesiastes admits that although humans try, they
cannot ultimately control what happens in life.

THE VALUE OF WISDOM

Wisdom in Ecclesiastes is not always viewed with suspicion. Of course,
the wisdom coming from God is to be preferred, but the Preacher acknowledges some merit in human wisdom: "So I turned to consider wisdom, madness and folly, for what will the man do who will come after
the king except what has already been done? And I saw that wisdom excels folly as light excels darkness" (Ecclesiastes 2:12-13).

The Preacher, in his efforts to move us toward faith in God, encourages the efforts of human ability and wisdom. What is objection-
able about human wisdom is the effort of humans to find meaning and
purpose in life without God. Otherwise, human wisdom, according
to the Preacher, has many advantages.

• *Human wisdom can give us success in the world.* Despite the vanity of toil and labor, it is wise to put forth our best efforts in our labors.
A commitment to the task at hand has a far greater chance of success
than if we approach it half-heartedly: "Whatever your hand finds to do,

verily, do it with all your might; for there is no activity or planning or wisdom in Sheol where you are going" (Ecclesiastes 9:10).

The grave (*Sheol*) is the end of all human enterprise. Common sense encourages us to seize the day and make life more pleasant and enjoyable. Paul challenged Christians to approach life with vision and vitality: "Therefore be careful how you walk, not as unwise men, but as wise, making the most of your time, because the days are evil" (Ephesians 5:15-16).

• *Human wisdom can preserve and protect our lives.* A common belief today is that knowledge is power. Our ability to think critically, to evaluate, to discern, and to make educated decisions can earn us the respect of others as well as make us wise to the ways of the world: "For wisdom is protection just as money is protection. But the advantage of knowledge is that wisdom preserves the lives of its possessors" (Ecclesiastes 7:12).

Jesus once told a parable about an unrighteous steward who was caught embezzling money from his master. Knowing he was about to lose his job, the unrighteous steward came up with a creative plan. Because he had no other skills, he knew he would need friends to fall back on. He called in his master's debtors and decreased their debts before he was fired, therefore causing them to be indebted to him as well. The steward's ingenious plan worked and impressed his former employer. Although not condoning the actions of the steward, Jesus commends his shrewdness. In fact, Jesus makes the point that the people of God should be just as wise in their dealings with spiritual matters (Luke 16:3-9).

• *Human wisdom can give us resolve.* Earl Nightingale, the granddaddy of motivational speaking, was known for offering this suggestion about how to tackle problems with skill. He said that any time we face an insurmountable problem we should take one sheet of paper and write at the top of the page what the problem is. Then on the rest of the paper, record every idea that comes to mind that could potentially provide a resolution. After this exercise, there should be a handful of ideas that could be implemented immediately. This simple exercise inspires the resolve to face and deal with any problem at hand. Wisdom breeds illumination: "Who is like the wise man and who knows the interpretation of a matter? A man's wisdom illumines him and causes his stern face to beam" (Ecclesiastes 8:1).

• *Human wisdom encourages resolve because it strengthens one's ability to see into a matter and view it from many angles.* Two heads are better than one; however, a person of wisdom possesses the insights of many minds: "Wisdom strengthens a wise man more than ten rulers who are in a city" (Ecclesiastes 7:19).

• *Human wisdom is better than brute strength.* At times diplomatic negotiation achieves what war cannot. Unfortunately, wisdom does not often receive the credit it deserves.

> Also this I came to see as wisdom under the sun, and it impressed me. There was a small city with few men in it and a great king came to it, surrounded it, and constructed large siegeworks against it. But there was found in it a poor wise man and he delivered the city by his wisdom. Yet no one remembered that poor man. So I said, "Wisdom is better than strength." But the wisdom of the poor man is despised and his words are not heeded. The words of the wise heard in quietness are better than the shouting of a ruler among fools. Wisdom is better than weapons of war, but one sinner destroys much good. (Ecclesiastes 9:13-18)

Although wisdom is preferred, obviously many do not desire it. As the passage declares, "One sinner destroys much good." In other words, the collateral damage of one fool is extensive. Why is wisdom so neglected by many people? The Preacher gives some insight into this dilemma: "Behold, I have found only this, that God made men upright, but they have sought out many devices" (Ecclesiastes 7:29). The cry of wisdom cannot be heard because of the roar of wickedness in the streets of the city.

• *Human wisdom can guide us.* The quest for knowledge and wisdom might be vanity; however, the quest allowed the Preacher to make that discovery! Ecclesiastes is a testimony to human wisdom's ability to discover how human wisdom is inadequate to provide the answers for human purpose:

> I said to myself, "Behold, I have magnified and increased wisdom more than all who were over Jerusalem before me; and

> my mind has observed a wealth of wisdom and knowledge."
> And I set my mind to know wisdom and to know madness
> and folly; I realized that this also is striving after wind. Because
> in much wisdom there is much grief, and increasing knowl-
> edge results in increasing pain. (Ecclesiastes 1:16-18)

Human wisdom must receive some credit for having discredited itself!

• *Human wisdom makes our labor fruitful.* Wisdom can help us build a legacy. The Preacher agrees with this truth. However, the tragedy is that those who may be the benefactors of the legacy may be fools: "When there is a man who has labored with wisdom, knowledge and skill, then he gives his legacy to one who has not labored with them. This too is vanity and a great evil" (Ecclesiastes 2:21).

Not every human being possesses wisdom. And no matter how much wisdom we may possess, it does not naturally follow that those who come after us will also possess it.

• *Human wisdom helps us evaluate life's experiences.* A wise person can see trouble ahead of him and can alter his course to avoid it. A wise person is able to learn from the mistakes of the past and can be better equipped not to repeat them in the future:

> I tested all this with wisdom, and I said, "I will be wise," but
> it was far from me. What has been is remote and exceedingly
> mysterious. Who can discover it? I directed my mind to know,
> to investigate, and to seek wisdom and an explanation, and
> to know the evil of folly and the foolishness of madness. And
> I discovered more bitter than death the woman whose heart
> is snares and nets, whose hands are chains. One who is pleas-
> ing to God will escape from her, but the sinner will be cap-
> tured by her. (Ecclesiastes 7:23-26)

The merits of human wisdom are impressive. We can see the appeal of living a life under the sun without any real accountability to God. After all, if human wisdom has the capacity to direct and shape our steps, then who needs God? This, of course, is the delusion of human wisdom. The whole story has yet to be told.

WISDOM'S VILLAINS: TIME AND CHANCE

Despite its merits, human wisdom is woefully inadequate to explain how and why the world behaves the way it does. The Preacher reveals the real villains of human wisdom, rendering it powerless: "I again saw under the sun that the race is not to the swift, and the battle is not to the warriors, and neither is bread to the wise, nor wealth to the discerning, nor favor to men of ability; for time and chance overtake them all" (Ecclesiastes 9:11).

Two elements of surprise over which human wisdom has no control are time and chance. They are the villains of human wisdom. Time represents how unpredictable life is. The uncertainty of time is a biblical theme often used to instill faith in God, not in human wisdom. Job states, "Man, who is born of woman, Is short-lived and full of turmoil" (Job 14:1). The New Testament book of James compares human life to a "vapor that appears for a little while then vanishes away" (4:14). The uncertainty of time is a "warrant for faith but also a death-blow for self-confidence" (Eaton 130).

The word "chance" alludes to life's unexpected surprises. God's call for the life of the rich farmer was unexpected. The farmer's wisdom – to build bigger barns so he could enjoy his remaining days in comfort – proved to be foolish. Chance, or more precisely God's intervention, nullified the farmer's wisdom.

The impact of time and chance can be seen in the ironies existing in life. The Preacher observes how several of these human ironies reveal the inadequacy of human wisdom.

• *The favored may lose.* The race does not always go to the swift. The old fable about the turtle and the hare shows this to be true. An upset comes when the unlikely opponent wins – the underdog, as many would say today.

• *The stronger may be defeated.* The Old Testament has many examples where this happened. The most notable one might be David's victory over the mighty Goliath of the Philistines (1 Samuel 17). Another example might be how Gideon's army of 300 defeated their enemy numbering in the thousands (Judges 7).

• *The wise may starve.* Having human wisdom does not guarantee prosperity.

• *The ablest may be poor.* The wise man who delivered a city by his wisdom was poor (Ecclesiastes 9:13-16).

• *The innocent may be ignored.* The classic story of Joseph illustrates this point. He was sold into slavery by his brothers, falsely accused by the wife of his master, and ignored in prison by those he helped (Genesis 37–41).

Time and chance neutralize the gains of human wisdom. According to the Preacher, time and chance are like predators: "Moreover, man does not know his time: like fish caught in a treacherous net, and birds trapped in a snare, so the sons of men are ensnared at an evil time when it suddenly falls on them" (Ecclesiastes 9:12).

We cannot escape the predator of time. The "evil time" in the above passage has two images. The first image is that of death. The Preacher encourages us to avoid immorality and other foolish behavior because they can lead to a premature death (Ecclesiastes 7:17). The second image is that of disaster. We cannot predict the type and the time of those unexpected surprises of life. Disaster forever lurks in the shadows:

> If no one knows what will happen, who can tell him when
> it will happen? No man has authority to restrain the wind
> with the wind, or authority over the day of death; and there
> is no discharge in the time of war, and evil will not deliver
> those who practice it. (Ecclesiastes 8:7-8)

No one has advance knowledge of his or her "evil time." The predator watches and waits; then at a time least expected, the predator makes his kill. Additionally, no one can escape his or her "evil time." The net and snare are traps prepared especially for prey. Such traps are effective and achieve their intended purpose. When the trap is set, the "evil time" comes abruptly, without warning and without mercy.

The only possible way to elude the villains of time and chance is to find refuge in the "hand of God." We do not know, nor can we know, what the future holds for us. This lack of knowledge and the uncertainty of life should compel every human being to trust in God: "For I have taken all this to my heart and explain it that righteous men, wise men, and their deeds are in the hand of God. Man does not know whether it will be love or hatred; anything awaits him" (Ecclesiastes 9:1).

QUESTIONS FOR PERSONAL AND GROUP REFLECTION

1. What are the benefits and the flaws of self-help or pop psychology books? Do you find any parallels between the benefits of wisdom as presented by the Preacher and pop psychology? What is the inherent weakness of human wisdom?

2. How have you benefited from human wisdom? Are human wisdom and common sense the same or different?

3. Describe the villains of human wisdom and how they affect it.

4. Describe some common ironies going against human wisdom. Can you think of other examples found in the Bible and in the world?

5. How is life like a snare or net? How do you plan for the unexpected things of life?

7

SEEKING CLARITY, FINDING CONFUSION

I cannot forecast to you the action of Russia.
It is a riddle wrapped in a mystery inside an enigma.
– Winston Churchill (Oct. 1, 1939)

[A]nd I saw every work of God, I concluded that man cannot
discover the work which has been done under the sun. Even
though man should seek laboriously, he will not discover; and
though the wise man should say, "I know," he cannot
discover. (Ecclesiastes 8:17)

The TV series, *Star Trek: The Next Generation*, introduced viewers to a new alien in the universe. In the pilot episode, this alien placed the human race on trial. His name was "Q." His alien race was also called "Q," and they lived in what they called the Q Continuum. In the TV series, Q, and all like him, were omnipotent beings. Q, like the mythological Greek gods, thought of the human race as a toy for his own amusement. He enjoyed mocking Captain Picard, the captain of the starship *Enterprise*. He referred to humans as beings who take from the universe but give nothing to it. Humans are a sorry excuse for a life form. The TV series had numerous episodes where Q appeared, taunting and teasing the crew of the *Enterprise*. A reader of Ecclesiastes might mistakenly conclude that God is somewhat like Q. Are we simply pawns in the hands of the omnipotent God of the universe? Or is there more to our existence?

Sometimes life is too confusing to understand. There is no clarity. Only God and faith in Him provides the mental clarity that humans need. Otherwise we're hopeless to make sense out of life.

IS GOD PLAYING GAMES?

The danger inherent in Ecclesiastes is to read sections as detachments from their contexts within the book. The Preacher's goal is to lead his readers to the fear of God (Ecclesiastes12:13-14). To achieve this purpose, the Preacher sets out to destroy not only the failure of human wisdom regarding life "under the sun" but also the human drive to seek out an explanation for every dilemma in life. Many things about life cannot be explained by human wisdom. We must ultimately concede that the activities of God can neither be explained nor avoided. The following questions give rise to curious enigmas about the God of the universe.

• *Does God delight in our frustrations?* We can easily get the impression God made the world in such a way as to confound human beings: "I set my mind to seek and explore by wisdom concerning all that has been done under heaven. It is a grievous task which God has given to the sons of men to be afflicted with" (Ecclesiastes 1:13).

The grievous task humans must face is the enigma of facing the problems of life. "God has given" is a phrase more accurately understood as a reference to a divine appointment. Each person must struggle with the trials of life. Just as Jeremiah was appointed as God's spokesman to the nation of Israel (Jeremiah 1:5), every human is divinely appointed with the task called life. Jeremiah could not run from his divine appointment, nor could he excuse himself from the obligation. God held him accountable as He also holds us accountable.

• *Does God play favorites?* How can God love all people equally and yet favor a special group of people?

> For to a person who is good in His sight He has given wisdom and knowledge and joy, while to the sinner He has given the task of gathering and collecting so that he may give to one who is good in God's sight. This too is vanity and striving after wind. (Ecclesiastes 2:26)

Again, the phrase "He has given" is an affirmation of God's prerogative. We live in God's universe, not in a universe humans have created. God does bless the faithful. The truth is God loves all people but not all people love Him in return. Consequently, God blesses the "good"; that is, the people who "fear Him." The vanity motif at the end of the verse seems to refer to the fruitless toil of the sinner. This makes sense in light of the fact that the sinner's life is viewed as taking place under the sun – apart from God. The blessing of God upon the righteous is a common teaching in the Old and New Testaments (Proverbs 13:22;

Matthew 5:5; 1 Corinthians 3:21; Hebrews 11:6; 1 Peter 3:11-12).

• *Does God purposely derail human industry?* We were introduced to the vanity of human toil in Chapter 1. The futility of labor continues to be a theme in Chapter 2. In Chapter 3, however, we may begin to wonder whether human labor is fruitless because God has somehow sabotaged or jinxed the system of sowing and reaping. "What profit is there to the worker from that in which he toils? I have seen the task which God has given the sons of men with which to occupy themselves" (Ecclesiastes 3:9-10).

In Ecclesiastes 3:10, the phrase "God has given" in this context is an acknowledgment of God's providential control over time. This passage is a reflection upon the poem about time in verses 2-8. The Preacher introduces the poem by affirming the times of every event as appointed times: "There is an appointed time for everything. And there is a time for every event under heaven" (v. 1).

The implication is that God controls the times and events; humans do not. Consequently, any effort to do so by human effort is fruitless. Despite such fruitlessness, humans still attempt to gain control. God, therefore, is not sabotaging the efforts of humans; rather, the efforts of humans are doomed to fail from the very beginning. The prophet Daniel affirmed God's control of time when God revealed to him the interpretation of a king's dream. "[I]t is He who changes the times and the epochs; He removes kings and establishes kings; He gives wisdom to wise men, And knowledge to men of understanding. It is He who reveals the profound and hidden things; He knows what is in the darkness, and the light dwells with Him" (Daniel 2:21-22).

• *Does God deceive?* Human beings appear to be helpless in their search for purpose in life. They feel compelled by a consuming drive to seek out a higher power. The Preacher also observes this natural desire within human beings: "He has made everything appropriate in its time. He has also set eternity in their heart, yet so that man will not find out the work which God has done from the beginning even to the end" (Ecclesiastes 3:11).

The phrase "He has also set" is an affirmation of God's creative power. "Eternity in their heart" corresponds to the nature of human creation – created in the image of God (Genesis 1:26) – and a person's inward

longing for God. While preaching in the city of Athens, Paul showed
how the human propensity of worship is an internal testimony of God's
existence. The Athenians, however, were misguided in their drive to
satisfy their longing to worship.

> "The God who made the world and all things in it, since He
> is Lord of heaven and earth, does not dwell in temples made
> with hands; neither is He served by human hands, ... He
> made from one, every nation of mankind to live on all the
> face of the earth, having determined their appointed times,
> and the boundaries of their habitation, that they should seek
> God, if perhaps they might grope for Him and find Him,
> though He is not far from each one of us; for in Him we live
> and move and exist, as even some of your own poets have
> said, 'For we also are His offspring.' " (Acts 17:24-28)

Paul said people were created to "seek God." This refers to the same
idea the Preacher means by "eternity in their hearts." God can be found
only through faith, not by human wisdom.

• *Does God treat us unfairly?* The difference between God playing
favorites and Him treating us unfairly is in the implied accusation against
God's nature of justice. We may wonder whether God administers equal
justice in the world after reading Ecclesiastes 6:1-2:

> There is an evil which I have seen under the sun and it is
> prevalent among men – a man to whom God has given rich-
> es and wealth and honor so that his soul lacks nothing of all
> that he desires, but God has not empowered him to eat from
> them, for a foreigner enjoys them. This is vanity and a se-
> vere affliction.

On the surface, one easily gets the impression God has treated the
man he has blessed unfairly or perhaps even cruelly. Here God blesses a person and then does not allow that person to enjoy the blessing
He gave. In context, the passage actually teaches the opposite.
Unfortunately, the arbitrary chapter divisions within the book can con-
ceal the broader context in which a passage of scripture is located. This
is one such place where the meaning is obscured because of the chapter division.

The broader context referring to the man mentioned in Ecclesiastes 6:1-2 stands in contrast to the one mentioned in 5:18-20:

> Here is what I have seen to be good and fitting: to eat, to drink and enjoy oneself in all one's labor in which he toils under the sun during the few years of his life which God has given him; for this is his reward. Furthermore, as for every man to whom God has given riches and wealth, He has also empowered him to eat from them and to receive his reward and rejoice in his labor; this is the gift of God. For he will not often consider the years of his life, because God keeps him occupied with the gladness of his heart.

Both passages together form a complete unit of thought. The man in 5:18-20 is blessed by God and is able to enjoy God's gifts because of his relationship with God. In contrast to this man is the man in 6:1-2 whom God has also blessed (which demonstrates the non-partiality of God's general blessings upon humankind), but because he does not fear God, he cannot enjoy life as God meant for it to be enjoyed. The phrases "God has given" and "God has not empowered" denote God's personal involvement in human affairs. The man unable to enjoy God's blessings is the man unable to see the purpose of life because he is without God. To amplify such wastefulness, the Preacher says a foreigner will ultimately enjoy this man's riches. We were previously introduced to the inability of a person to control the legacy he leaves behind in Ecclesiastes 2:18-23.

These enigmas about God really turn out to be misunderstandings about the message of Ecclesiastes. God is not manipulative or menacing. On the contrary, He is a giving God.

GOD'S ACTIVITY ON OUR BEHALF

God has blessed humankind. And the Preacher wants to show us how humankind's true joy is linked to the hand of God: "There is nothing better for a man than to eat and drink and tell himself that his labor is good. This also I have seen, that it is from the hand of God. For who can eat and who can have enjoyment without Him?" (Ecclesiastes 2:24-25).

Without God, humankind is at a loss for real meaning for life. The two greatest gifts from God are the two greatest needs of every human. The human need for joy is the first gift. Joy means more than happiness and describes a state of existence independent from the environment or circumstances in life: "[M]oreover, that every man who eats and drinks sees good in all his labor – it is the gift of God" (Ecclesiastes 3:13).

Eating and drinking are tokens of a contented and joyful life. This is so because of a profound new factor at work – the sovereignty of God over our lives. The good life is in opposition to the secular life. "Secularism gives way to theism, pessimism to optimism, human autonomy to human faith" (Eaton 82).

The second need of humans is peace. This need describes a state of being within as well as providing a vantage point from which to see the world. To be at peace with ourselves and at peace with our neighbor are what the Preacher refers to as the gladness of heart.

> Furthermore, as for every man to whom God has given riches and wealth, He has also empowered him to eat from them and to receive his reward and rejoice in his labor; this is the gift of God. For he will not often consider the years of his life, because God keeps him occupied with the gladness of his heart. (Ecclesiastes 5:19-20)

In the New Testament, the words "grace" (joy) and "peace" become a Christian salutation (1 Corinthians 1:3; 2 Corinthians 1:2; Galatians 1:3; Ephesians 1:2).

GOD: BOTH PERSONAL AND TRANSCENDENT

One of the purposes of Ecclesiastes is to present God as involved in a personal way in the affairs of people and removed from the arena of this world. In other words, God is both personal and transcendent. God's transcendence exposes the real enigmas about Him. Perhaps the thought is if human wisdom could explain God, then God would be inferior to the wisdom of man. God, however, is above and beyond the scope of human wisdom. The Preacher succeeds in portraying a God shrouded in mystery.

• *God's plans cannot be fully known.* What we know about God is what has been revealed. Anything more is mere speculation and an exercise in futility: "He has made everything appropriate in its time. He has also set eternity in their heart, yet so that man will not find out the work which God has done from the beginning even to the end" (Ecclesiastes 3:11).

In many respects, the work of God will always be a mystery. As Moses said long ago, "The secret things belong to the Lord our God, but the things revealed belong to us and to our sons forever, that we may observe all the words of this law" (Deuteronomy 29:29).

The activities of God cannot be fully discovered. The Preacher said he saw every work of God and yet he did not see the work of God. His statement almost seems contradictory. Here is how it reads in context:

> [A]nd I saw every work of God, I concluded that man cannot discover the work which has been done under the sun. Even though man should seek laboriously, he will not discover; and though the wise man should say, "I know," he cannot discover. (Ecclesiastes 8:17)

The excessive claims by some people who believe they know the activities of God are without substance. The New Testament teaches how in Jesus there is a sense in which we can know the activities of God. Outside of Jesus, however, God remains a mystery (John 1:18; 1 Corinthians 2:10-16; 13:12).

• *God's purposes cannot be altered.* The Preacher has also shown how we cannot change or manipulate the will of God to suit our own purposes: "Consider the work of God, For who is able to straighten what He has bent?" (Ecclesiastes 7:13; 1:15).

The answer is obvious, of course – no one is able to change the will of God. In Ecclesiastes, God is a great mystery and His works are marvels to behold: "Just as you do not know the path of the wind and how bones are formed in the womb of the pregnant woman, so you do not know the activity of God who makes all things" (Ecclesiastes 11:5).

Is God like the omnipotent alien called "Q"? Does He manipulate and tease us for His own pleasure? The Preacher has shown how the mystery shrouding God's will is not a divine ruse to stifle the human spirit; rather, it is the Preacher's way of showing us how glorious and wondrous the God of the universe is.

QUESTIONS FOR PERSONAL AND GROUP REFLECTION

1. How have you worked through some of the mystery surrounding God's actions? In what ways are the Preacher's observations about God similar to your own?

2. What does it mean when the Preacher says God has set eternity in our hearts? How could this thought serve as evidence for God's existence?

3. Describe the blessings God offers to all people. Why do people not receive them?

4. How is God both personal and transcendent? Why is it important for God to be both?

5. Explain how important the context of a passage is in understanding its message. Find an example from this chapter and discuss it.

8

SEEKING OPPORTUNITIES, FINDING DEAD ENDS

*At birth our death is sealed, and our end is consequent
upon our beginning.– Marcus Manilius (First Century A.D.)*

A time to give birth, and a time to die. (Ecclesiastes 3:2)

The late Dr. W.B. West, professor of Greek and New Testament studies at a number of universities, was known for having a plaque prominently displayed on his large desk. You would expect the plaque would have borne his name. The words written in gold, however, were actually a Greek phrase. It read "ωρα εκε δοξαν." The translation is: "An hour has glory." This was Dr. West's way of encouraging his Greek students to take every available opportunity to learn and study their Greek exercises. The plaque also represented Dr. West's goal in life – to seize the moment and use it to the glory of God.

In contrast to the positive emphasis Dr. West placed upon time, the Preacher in Ecclesiastes presents the darker side of time. The poem on time in Chapter 3 is one of the most famous and infamous sections of Ecclesiastes. The Preacher sees time not as an opportunity to seize but as a trap where humans are caught in the appointed times and cannot do anything to free themselves. Time will run its course, and all people have played its game. How then can we adjust and participate joyfully under the tyranny of time?

THE TIMING OF TIME

The best way to evaluate Ecclesiastes 3:1-11 is to place it within the context of Ecclesiastes. Many readers get the impression that the

Preacher is providing a principle of life that justifies certain human activities. Yet, it seems a bit suspect to find justification for hatred and war. Rather, the poem is an illustration of how humans are unable to control the activities and the outcomes of life. Humans are living within a cycle that forever runs its course. The poem stresses two themes about God and humankind.

The first theme is the authority of God over time. The inability to control time is based upon the fact that we are inside time and subject to its laws, not outside time, separate and autonomous. Ecclesiastes 3:1 and 11 form an inclusion stressing the transcendence and sovereignty of God over time: "There is an appointed time for everything. And there is a time for every event under heaven. ... He has made everything appropriate in its time." The phrase "appointed time" and the word "event" underscore the authority of God and refer to how He created the world.

Although all things appear to be pre-determined, there is the element of human free-will, which is also a part of God's creation and the cause of much human misery. For instance, the Preacher observes how injustice, injury and iniquity are matters of human resolve and determination: "Furthermore, I have seen under the sun that in the place of justice there is wickedness, and in the place of righteousness there is wickedness" (Ecclesiastes 3:16); "Behold, I have found only this, that God made men upright, but they have sought out many devices" (7:29); "All this I have seen and applied my mind to every deed that has been done under the sun wherein a man has exercised authority over another man to his hurt" (8:9); "Wisdom is better than weapons of war, but one sinner destroys much good" (9:18).

The Preacher reinforces God's authority over time by noting how all people are at the mercy of time: "What profit is there to the worker from that in which he toils? I have seen the task which God has given the sons of men with which to occupy themselves" (Ecclesiastes 3:9-10).

The toils of the worker are to be understood as attempts to override the mechanism of time. However, humans are pictured as subservient to the elements of the activities of time. Human time is occupied by the events of time, and these events or time's laws cannot be reprogrammed. God has given humans the task of living within the parameters of time.

The second theme of the poem on time relates to our inadequacy to control it. There are a number of reasons why we cannot circumvent time:

• *We cannot predict time.* The events of time – both positive and negative – cannot be known beforehand: "For there is a proper time and procedure for every delight, when a man's trouble is heavy upon him. If no one knows what will happen, who can tell him when it will happen?" (Ecclesiastes 8:6-7).

The trouble weighing heavily upon man refers to the perplexities, frustrations and ignorance about the future. No one can see into the future by intuition, nor can anyone gain an advantage about what the future holds by seeking counsel from his neighbor. As the Preacher says, no one knows: "Yet the fool multiplies words. No man knows what will happen, and who can tell him what will come after him?" (Ecclesiastes 10:14).

• *We cannot control time.* As stated before, we live within time, not outside time. Our world exists within the boundaries of time and must conform and flow along with the currents of time. We may not like the trap we're caught in; nevertheless, we're helpless to find an escape: "Whatever exists has already been named, and it is known what man is; for he cannot dispute with him who is stronger than he is" (Ecclesiastes 6:10).

• *We cannot explain time.* Human wisdom is at a loss to make sense of the world of time. This is the Preacher's way of moving us to faith in the God who is beyond time. Before faith can occur, however, the Preacher must press us into admitting our complete surrender to the tyrant of time. "I tested all this with wisdom, and I said, 'I will be wise,' but it was far from me. What has been is remote and exceedingly mysterious. Who can discover it?" (Ecclesiastes 7:23-24).

THE SEASONS OF TIME

Now that we have seen how all people are at the mercy of time, the poem on time begins to reveal several sets of contrasts showing how human life exists on a set timeline. Often these events of life are understood as the seasons of time.

The first season relates to the limits of human existence within the world of time. The human experience has a beginning and an end: "A time to give birth, and a time to die" (Ecclesiastes 3:2).

The Preacher views the time span from birth to death as a period of fragile futility (Ecclesiastes 6:12). This first set of contrasts introduces the form for the rest of the poem and also provides the interpretive clue to the poem. The key to interpretation relates to the first set of contrasts: Both the beginning and the ending of human existence are beyond human control. No person can predict the time of his birth or the time of his death. Other human events that follow are likewise unpredictable.

The second season relates to the events within the human experience. The next series of contrasts are to be understood as the general events common to all human experience:

> A time to plant, and a time to uproot what is planted. A time to kill, and a time to heal; A time to tear down, and a time to build up. A time to weep, and a time to laugh; A time to mourn, and a time to dance. A time to throw stones, and a time to gather stones; A time to embrace, and a time to shun embracing. A time to search, and a time to give up as lost; A time to keep, and a time to throw away. A time to tear apart, and a time to sew together; A time to be silent, and a time to speak. A time to love, and a time to hate; A time for war, and a time for peace. (Ecclesiastes 3:2-8)

The above events cover a span of human emotions, both positive and negative. These events, however, should not be assigned any moral significance. All of them are proper activities along our timeline. This cannot, however, be the claim for immoral behavior:

> Notably, the poem does not include "a time to be wise and a time to be foolish"; or "a time to be righteous and a time to be wicked"; or "a time to fear God and a time to sin"; or "a time to be lazy and time to be diligent" [or] "a time to oppress and a time to do justice." Although there are times for both pleasant and unpleasant activities, Qohelet [Hebrew word meaning preacher or teacher, GSG] never suggest that there is a proper time for injustice or wickedness. (Murphy and Huwiler 188)

These events of time stress the unexpected nature of their occurrence. When the appointed time (or human experience) does come, we are to understand it as part of life. We do not choose the event; the event chooses us. We must ride the roller coaster of time while facing all of the emotions coming along with the ride – pleasant or unpleasant.

ADAPTING TO THE EVENTS OF TIME

Because we live within the framework of time from which no one can escape, it would seem reasonable for us to learn how to have a proper frame of mind toward time. According to the Preacher, that would consist of the following principles:

• *Accept the mystery of time.* The Preacher holds before us the elusiveness of time. Because time and its events are unpredictable and uncertain, a cloud of mystery envelopes the seasons of time. By accepting the uncertainties of life, we can lessen their impact when they do arise.

> Consider the work of God, For who is able to straighten what He has bent? In the day of prosperity be happy, But in the day of adversity consider – God has made the one as well as the other So that man may not discover anything that will be after him. (Ecclesiastes 7:13-14)

• *Anticipate the misery of time.* If we have ever held unreasonable expectations about what we should receive from life, we've fallen prey to one of life's greatest deceptions. The inability to accept the bad in life can cause the unpleasant experiences to color the good things life has to offer. Life not only has hills but also valleys.

> "Behold, I have discovered this," says the Preacher, "adding one thing to another to find an explanation, which I am still seeking but have not found. I have found one man among a thousand, but I have not found a woman among all these. Behold, I have found only this, that God made men upright, but they have sought out many devices." (Ecclesiastes 7:27-29)

The New Testament takes the position that experiences in life often involve suffering and misery: "For we know that the whole creation groans and suffers the pains of childbirth together until now" (Romans 8:22).

• *Acknowledge the amusement of time.* One of the hardest disciplines to learn when experiencing the peaks and valleys of life is the ability to enjoy the good times when they occur. You've probably discovered how you have a natural inclination of allowing the bad experiences of life to eclipse any good experiences. Each day offers both bad and good experiences. The ability to acknowledge the good along with the bad is a way in which the burden of time becomes lighter.

> Go then, eat your bread in happiness, and drink your wine with a cheerful heart; for God has already approved your works. Let your clothes be white all the time, and let not oil be lacking on your head. Enjoy life with the woman whom you love all the days of your fleeting life which He has given to you under the sun; for this is your reward in life, and in your toil in which you have labored under the sun. (Ecclesiastes 9:7-9)

The psalmist uttered a prayer to God asking for the discipline to see the balance between both good and bad experiences in life: "Make us glad according to the days Thou hast afflicted us, And the years we have seen evil" (Psalm 90:15).

• *Anchor to the Master for all time.* The best possible solution for dealing with the enigma of time is to have faith in the God who controls it. The Preacher has achieved his goal if he has compelled us to surrender to the will of God: "For I have taken all this to my heart and explain it that righteous men, wise men, and their deeds are in the hand of God. Man does not know whether it will be love or hatred; anything awaits him" (Ecclesiastes 9:1).

A person who trusts in God removes the mystery of time for the simple reason that such a person does not concern himself with life's uncertainties: "My times are in Thy hand; Deliver me from the hand of my enemies, and from those who persecute me" (Psalm 31:15).

Consequently, faith in God will help us face the doubts, fears, frustrations and burdens of life with a spirit of confidence instead of a spirit of defeat. God is truly the God of time management.

For I consider that the sufferings of this present time are not worthy to be compared with the glory that is to be revealed to us. For the anxious longing of the creation waits eagerly for the revealing of the sons of God. For the creation was subjected to futility, not of its own will, but because of Him who subjected it, in hope that the creation itself also will be set free from its slavery to corruption into the freedom of the glory of the children of God. (Romans 8:18-21)

DISCUSSIONS FOR PERSONAL AND GROUP REFLECTION

1. In what ways could the poem on time in Ecclesiastes 3:1-11 be abused?

2. What is the significance of the poem on time? What is the Preacher's purpose, and does he succeed in his purpose?

3. How can time be your enemy and your friend?

4. In what ways can you relate to the experiences in the poem on time? How would you describe the arrival of these experiences – shocking, unexpected, anticipated, etc.?

5. What advice does the Preacher give for coping with time?

9

SEEKING ANSWERS, FINDING QUESTIONS

The Almighty has His own purposes. – Abraham Lincoln

What then is the advantage to a man? For who knows what is good for a man during his lifetime, during the few years of his futile life? (Ecclesiastes 6:11-12)

The word "religion" means "to bind back." Religion seeks to communicate to humanity the teachings of God, revealing the way back to Him. Showing the world the way back to God is a sobering task. Unfortunately, religion often misrepresents God, distorting His message and at times dismissing it altogether. Religion should seek to resolve questions about human existence and purpose. Questions about life and death are usually at the top of humanity's list of concerns. The Preacher takes a look at these very important religious issues and, at times, challenges religious tradition.

In the wisdom literature of the Old Testament, Jewish orthodoxy has firm footing. Traditional beliefs such as the value of life, the need for wisdom, the blessings of God on the righteous, and God's judgment against the wicked are common themes, particularly in Psalms and Proverbs. The Preacher challenges some of these traditional beliefs as he reports what he observes in the world. Although he would agree with the traditional themes of Judaism, he underscores the fact that traditional religious resolutions are often shallow and misleading.

THE TRUTH ABOUT LIFE

When we read Ecclesiastes, we notice certain disparities between what the Preacher may believe and what he actually observes in the world.

These mixed messages create doubt and uncertainty.

• *The first disparity is seen in the Preacher's observations about wisdom.* Wisdom is a path that leads to security and ensures success with the added benefit of keeping us from acting foolishly. "For wisdom is protection just as money is protection. But the advantage of knowledge is that wisdom preserves the lives of its possessors" (Ecclesiastes 7:12).

Although wisdom is preferred and encouraged as a way of life, the Preacher concludes there is really no benefit from possessing it. "Then I said to myself, 'As is the fate of the fool, it will also befall me. Why then have I been extremely wise?' So I said to myself, 'This too is vanity' " (Ecclesiastes 2:15).

The meaning of wisdom is somewhat unclear at first. Wisdom is better; wisdom is not better. Which is it?

• *The second disparity exists in the Preacher's discussion about life.* The Preacher is no doubt familiar with the view that humans were created in the image of God. Because humans were God's highest creation, they received special recognition above other creations. Yet, Ecclesiastes stands as a treatise on the vanity of life. Human life, according to the Preacher, is not as noble as we might believe. The beginning statement is enough to shock any reader having traditional religious grounding: " 'Vanity of vanities,' says the Preacher, 'Vanity of vanities! All is vanity' " (Ecclesiastes 1:2).

On the other hand, the Preacher speaks highly of life and even goes so far as to suggest how enjoyable and satisfying life is: "And I have seen that nothing is better than that man should be happy in his activities, for that is his lot. For who will bring him to see what will occur after him?" (Ecclesiastes 3:22).

Life is vanity; life is not vanity. How can life be empty and fulfilling at the same time? Is the Preacher contradicting himself?

• *The third disparity centers on human knowledge.* The Preacher claims he knows certain things about God. "Although a sinner does evil a hundred times and may lengthen his life, still I know that it will be well for those who fear God, who fear Him openly" (Ecclesiastes 8:12).

What is intriguing about his statement of confidence is throughout the book we read comments disparaging knowledge: "Even though man should seek laboriously, he will not discover; and though the wise man should say, 'I know,' he cannot discover" (Ecclesiastes 8:17).

How is it the Preacher says humans can know and in the same chapter assert humans cannot know? Again, is the Preacher sending mixed messages?

• *A fourth disparity has to do with labor.* Human industry is praised and often presented in a favorable light: "There is nothing better for a man than to eat and drink and tell himself that his labor is good. This also I have seen, that it is from the hand of God" (Ecclesiastes 2:24).

Human toil appears to have the blessing of God. However, the first major section of Ecclesiastes is a poem about the futility of human labor. The poem opens with a question that appears to be at odds with the passage above: "What advantage does man have in all his work Which he does under the sun?" (Ecclesiastes 1:3).

The context of the labor poem requires a negative answer to the above question. Absolutely no advantage to human labor is under the sun. Now we face a dilemma: labor is good; labor is not good. There seems to be a contradiction between what the Preacher believes and what he actually observes.

• *The fifth disparity is the subject of money.* From all indications, money or material things can be hazards to human spiritual growth. This is an orthodox way of looking at the material world. In light of this, it's puzzling to read the following words about money in the book of Ecclesiastes: "Men prepare a meal for enjoyment, and wine makes life merry, and money is the answer to everything" (10:19).

Many a prophet and preacher would have difficulty proclaiming money is the answer to a person's most inner needs. Would not teachers rather jump to a more traditional view found in an earlier section in Ecclesiastes? "He who loves money will not be satisfied with money, nor he who loves abundance with its income. This too is vanity" (Ecclesiastes 5:10).

Avoiding the tension about money in no way helps us deal honestly with what we find in the text. The contrast is there. Money is the answer; money is not the answer. Both statements cannot be right, can they?

• *The sixth disparity relates to the all-important subject of human purpose.* Discovering purpose in life is a top priority to a lot of people.

Without purpose, humans are adrift, meandering about with no real aim. According to the Preacher, we'll soon see how human purpose is found in faithfully serving God: "The conclusion, when all has been heard, is: fear God and keep His commandments, because this applies to every person" (Ecclesiastes 12:13).

However, before the obvious religious stance is proclaimed, the Preacher has demonstrated very effectively how humans have no real purpose in life.

> For there are many words which increase futility. What then is the advantage to a man? For who knows what is good for a man during his lifetime, during the few years of his futile life? He will spend them like a shadow. For who can tell a man what will be after him under the sun? (Ecclesiastes 6:11-12)

Describing man's life as being "like a shadow" highlights the transitory nature of human existence. A shadow is a figure of insecurity. The negative statements about human purpose are astounding. Humans do not know what is good about their lives, nor should anyone really care. How then can humans have a purpose to their existence when their existence lacks purpose?

KEY WORDS

We may get the impression the Preacher is saying one thing but meaning something else. The mixed messages, however, are not inconsistent with the realities of life. People who believe in God recognize that the answers to many questions are not all that simple. Life is complicated, and many variables are unknown. Faith is actually a place between two points of tension. For example, wisdom can be both a blessing and a curse, depending upon how we use it. The wisdom leading one astray from his or her Creator is ultimately vain no matter if wisdom has its worldly advantages. The same is true with money. Money is a tool used by both good and evil people. Money can become an object of human greed or a blessing for taking care of human needs. It all depends on the attitude we have toward it. The Preacher is not sending mixed messages; rather, he is presenting two polar opposites or ways of human life – the futility of living under the sun or the fulfillment of living as a God-fearer.

This distinction becomes clear when observing some key words the Preacher draws upon to make his point. These key words represent major life themes.

• *The first key word about life is "profit."* A synonym for this word is "advantage." Both terms are used in Ecclesiastes. The terms "profit" and "advantage" refer to what is "left over." The thought is that people without God cannot create a surplus – there is no profit. This is the meaning of the word "advantage" in Ecclesiastes 1:3. People without God are in the red.

• *The second key word about life is "lot."* The words "portion," "share" and "legacy" (Ecclesiastes 2:21; although the text illustrates a negative aspect about the future, it does speak highly of the worker who leaves a legacy) are sometimes used in its place. This term describes what God has granted to human beings. The human lot is a way of expressing a person's slice of the pie. The term "lot" is always used in Ecclesiastes in a positive way. It represents what is good in life when people yield to the will of God. "And I have seen that nothing is better than that man should be happy in his activities, for that is his lot. For who will bring him to see what will occur after him?" (Ecclesiastes 3:22).

• *The third key word about life is "toil" or "labor."* This term is primarily negative in Ecclesiastes, referring, of course, to our efforts without God at work, and to life in general. "For what does a man get in all his labor and in his striving with which he labors under the sun? Because all his days his task is painful and grievous; even at night his mind does not rest. This too is vanity" (Ecclesiastes 2:22-23).

• *The fourth key word about life is "joy" or "pleasure."* We are encouraged by the Preacher to find some joy in life. Lasting joy and pleasure are gifts from God to humans.

> The light is pleasant, and it is good for the eyes to see the sun. Indeed, if a man should live many years, let him rejoice in them all, and let him remember the days of darkness, for they shall be many. Everything that is to come will be futility. Rejoice, young man, during your childhood, and let

your heart be pleasant during the days of young manhood. And follow the impulses of your heart and the desires of your eyes. Yet know that God will bring you to judgment for all these things. So, remove vexation from your heart and put away pain from your body, because childhood and the prime of life are fleeting. (Ecclesiastes 11:7-10)

THE TRUTH ABOUT DEATH

Is there life after death? In Ecclesiastes, death and the grave (or Sheol) are important subjects. In fact, the Preacher maintains the view that life is vain because the grave is the great equalizer. The deaths of animals and humans, the wise and the foolish, and the rich and the poor are the same. "For the fate of the sons of men and the fate of beasts is the same. As one dies so does the other; indeed, they all have the same breath and there is no advantage for man over beast, for all is vanity. All go to the same place. All came from the dust and all return to the dust" (Ecclesiastes 3:19-20; cf. 2:12-17; 9:2-3; Psalm 49:1-12; 73:17-22).

The same "fate," as the Preacher would put it, awaits them all. This underscores the vanity of life. The Preacher uses the subject of death to raise questions about life after death. The only hope beyond the grave is found in the fear of the Lord; otherwise, in all practical purposes, the grave marks the end of human activity and erases any meaning we might have found while alive.

What about life after death? The Preacher appears to express doubt in an afterlife: "Who knows that the breath of man ascends upward and the breath of the beast descends downward to the earth?" (Ecclesiastes 3:21).

Yet, in context, the Preacher says the afterlife has no practical meaning to the godless (Ecclesiastes 3:18-19; 9:4-6). Life after death is meaningful to those who fear God. "[T]hen the dust will return to the earth as it was, and the spirit will return to God who gave it" (12:7; Genesis 3:19).

In the Preacher's discussion about old age is a hint of eternal existence with God in what is referred to as an "eternal home": "Furthermore, men are afraid of a high place and of terrors on the road; the almond tree blossoms, the grasshopper drags himself along, and the caperberry is ineffective. For man goes to his eternal home while mourners go about in the street" (Ecclesiastes 12:5; cf. Psalm 49:13-20; 2 Timothy 1:10).

For the person who fears and obeys God, hope extends beyond the grave. In contrast, the person who rejects God is of no account or as Paul would say in the New Testament: "without hope ... without God" (2 Thessalonians 1:7-9).

THE TRUTH ABOUT REWARD AND PUNISHMENT

The law of retribution is a technical way of referring to the principle of rewards and punishments. A traditional belief is that God always rewards righteousness and always punishes wickedness. However, the Preacher gives the impression that traditional belief clashes with what we may actually find in the real world.

Inequities run rampant in life. Good people on occasions are oppressed and wicked people flourish. People of religious conviction may fall into a state of disillusionment when witnessing such inequities and ponder why God does not seem too involved in resolving them. The Preacher does not reveal anything the people of God have not noticed before. The only difference is that the Preacher expresses what many religious people think but are afraid to say.

> I have seen everything during my lifetime of futility; there is a righteous man who perishes in his righteousness, and there is a wicked man who prolongs his life in his wickedness. (Ecclesiastes 7:15)

> There is futility which is done on the earth, that is, there are righteous men to whom it happens according to the deeds of the wicked. On the other hand, there are evil men to whom it happens according to the deeds of the righteous. I say that this too is futility. (8:14; cf. Psalm 73:1-6; Job 21:1-16)

Life under the sun is not always equitable. However, the people of God have every reason to have faith in God's justice. The Preacher shows the reality of what life is like, but the people of God must remember their timeline runs well beyond the grave. Because God's people take the longer view of time, they yield to the justice of God knowing that the inequities of life will eventually be corrected. "I said to myself, 'God will judge both the righteous man and the wicked man,' for a time for every matter and for every deed is there" (Ecclesiastes 3:17; cf. 11:9; 12:13; Romans 12:19, 21; 1 Peter 2:21-23).

The Preacher has addressed the three big issues of humankind – life, death and reward and punishment. What the Preacher has achieved is to provide a context from which to understand what the religion of God is all about. Sight must give way to faith. And when we fear God, struggling with life's dilemmas is not as difficult because we take the long view of the future instead of the short view of life ending at the grave.

QUESTIONS FOR PERSONAL AND GROUP REFLECTION

1. Should orthodox beliefs ever be questioned or challenged? What purpose would such a challenge serve?

2. Discuss the disparities that exist between what you may believe and what you actually observe. Begin with the list in this chapter and then move on to others you can think of. Are these disparities true contradictions? If not, how do you harmonize them?

3. How is a belief in God profitable? How is the Word of God profitable? Read 2 Timothy 3:16-17.

4. How does the Preacher use these terms: lot, labor and joy? Can you find similar thoughts in the New Testament?

5. The Preacher asserts good people may suffer and evil people may prosper. How does the Preacher reconcile this issue? How could you use Ecclesiastes as a tool to explain the problem of evil in the world?

10

SEEKING REASON, FINDING INSANITY

There is always inequity in life. ... Life is unfair.
– John F. Kennedy (March 21, 1962)

Furthermore, I have seen under the sun that in the place of
justice there is wickedness, and in the place of righteousness
there is wickedness. (Ecclesiastes 3:16)

Clint was my best friend in high school. I credit his father, Don, for motivating me to be a preacher of the gospel. In fact, the whole family made such an impact upon my life that I spent most of my time during my junior and senior years at their house! Because Clint and I were members of the same congregation, we had a special connection with each other. When I got the crazy idea one summer day about driving from Dallas, Texas, to Montgomery, Ala., to see Faulkner University, I asked Clint to come with me. He did without hesitation. What a trip we had! We have some of the funniest stories to tell about our week-long trip – stories we have told and laughed about at times until we finally collapsed from hilarious exhaustion!

Clint was diagnosed with cancer the year after our trip. He changed, his parents changed, and I changed. His illness was difficult to accept. Clint was a preacher's kid, and his dad was my mentor. As a preacher's family, they ministered to many people, and now they were suffering, hurting and asking, "Why?" Feelings of anger, doubt, fear and confusion were their constant companions. Clint was in his prime – a handsome, muscular and funny person. His chemotherapy treatments changed all of that. He lost his hair, shrank in size, and became withdrawn. I was with them and saw all the ups and downs as they experienced them. Bad things shouldn't happen to good people like these;

they don't deserve it! My faith encountered one of its greatest challenges that year.

Clint is healthy again. His treatments were successful. But the things we all learned that year were profound. We tried to make sense of it all, but there was no sense to make of it. We were at the mercy of life and, therefore, placed ourselves in the hand of God.

Inequities exist in life. Much of life, in fact, is troublesome. The Preacher in Ecclesiastes spares no emotion when describing how life is unfair and sometimes cruel. In a perfect world, life would follow a definitive path of constant self-improvement. However, we do not live in a perfect world. According to Ecclesiastes, experiences like Clint's were some of the things about life that grieved the Preacher.

HUMAN OPTIMISM

We must look carefully and thoroughly at the text of Ecclesiastes to find any sections that contain a spirit of optimism. However, it takes little effort to notice how pessimistic the Preacher is about life under the sun.

• *Youthful Vigor.* One of the objects of his scorn is youthful vigor. According to the Preacher, young people had better enjoy the days of their youth before those days come to an abrupt end.

> Rejoice, young man, during your childhood, and let your heart be pleasant during the days of young manhood. And follow the impulses of your heart and the desires of your eyes. ... So, remove vexation from your heart and put away pain from your body, because childhood and the prime of life are fleeting. (Ecclesiastes 11:9-10)

• *Age of Despair.* Youthful vigor quickly gives way to the age of despair.

> Remember also your Creator in the days of your youth, before the evil days come and the years draw near when you will say, "I have no delight in them"; before the sun, the light, the moon, and the stars are darkened, and clouds return after the rain. (Ecclesiastes 12:1-2)

The "evil days" that suddenly come represent sad or distressing times. Some days the weight of the world is borne upon our shoulders. The Preacher emphasizes how important it is to form a relationship with God early in life. People should begin the path of fearing God early and make that path a habit for the rest of their lives. The commitment we make by remembering the Creator will fortify our faith against the eventual evil days. The darkening of the sun, light, moon and stars represents our fading capacity for joy. The cycle of life will continue with its peaks and valleys for the clouds of trouble will return again.

• *Age of Decline*. Following the age of despair is the age of decline. In the cycle of human life, the pride of youth has but a short life span. Once the body reaches its prime in the days of youth, it quickly begins to break down. The glory of youth fades as the body becomes weak.

> [I]n the day that the watchmen of the house tremble, and mighty men stoop, the grinding ones stand idle because they are few, and those who look through windows grow dim; and the doors on the street are shut as the sound of the grinding mill is low, and one will arise at the sound of the bird, and all the daughters of song will sing softly. Furthermore, men are afraid of a high place and of terrors on the road; the almond tree blossoms, the grasshopper drags himself along, and the caperberry is ineffective. For man goes to his eternal home while mourners go about in the street. (Ecclesiastes 12:3-5)

The symbolism the Preacher uses to describe the process of growing old is fascinating. Although the meaning is uncertain, the following represents a sensible interpretation when the above text is considered in its context. Human arms are referred to as the "watchman of the house." Once upon a time the arms were strong and able to defend the house, but now they have lost their strength and therefore "tremble." Legs are identified under the figure of "mighty men." Legs are a figure of strength in biblical literature (Psalm 147:10). The "grinding ones standing idle" refers to the deterioration of teeth. Over time the teeth become fewer in number. "Windows" symbolize eyes. Unfortunately, as we age, the eyes become weak or as the text says, "dim." Also accompanying the age of decline will be sleeplessness, hearing loss, new fears, and restricted movement.

• *Age of Death.* The next stage following the period of decline is the age of death. Death is inevitable and certain. The irony is that humans are born to die: "Remember Him before the silver cord is broken and the golden bowl is crushed, the pitcher by the well is shattered and the wheel at the cistern is crushed" (Ecclesiastes 12:6).

Death, according to the Preacher, is the climax of life. At some point in time, death occurs, and life's support is removed. Again, the Preacher draws upon some unique images to give a visual picture of death. Because the "silver cord" holding the "golden bowl" breaks, the bowl is released and destroyed by the fall. The apparatus that supports the pitcher and allows it to be lowered into the well or cistern to draw out water breaks, and both the wheel and the pitcher fall to the bottom of the well and are crushed.

• *Age of Decay.* Once death has occurred, the age of decay takes over. The body begins to return to its original form and becomes again the dust of the earth. "[T]hen the dust will return to the earth as it was, and the spirit will return to God who gave it. 'Vanity of vanities,' says the Preacher, 'all is vanity!'" (Ecclesiastes 12:7-8).

The word "dust" should remind us of what God said about the human body in Genesis: "By the sweat of your face You shall eat bread, Till you return to the ground, Because from it you were taken; For you are dust, And to dust you shall return" (Genesis 3:19).

The whole aging process is troublesome to the Preacher. He concludes his discussion about life by repeating his introduction – "all is vanity." Certainly, no comfort is extended to people in the aging process if they are living apart from God. However, there is a comfort for those who fear God – the comfort of knowing death is not the end. Despite this comforting thought, we must still go through the process of aging.

HUMAN OPULENCE

Another grievance the Preacher has about life is placed against human opulence and greed. The Preacher does not condemn human gain and wealth; rather, he shows his disappointment with how people become consumed and enslaved to material things. To warn his readers against greed, the Preacher identifies several negative results of money and wealth.

• *Why can't we be satisfied with money?* Because we'll forever long for just a little bit more. "He who loves money will not be satisfied with money, nor he who loves abundance with its income. This too is vanity" (Ecclesiastes 5:10).

• *Why do people think if they had money it would not corrupt them?* This is the trap humans set for themselves. Money, of course, is neither good nor bad, but there is an obvious side effect to having it and a definite state of trouble created by longing for it.

• *Why does our popularity increase when we have money?* It is not enough for us to fight the battle of greed and contentment, but we must also fight the battle of instant popularity. "When good things increase, those who consume them increase. So what is the advantage to their owners except to look on?" (Ecclesiastes 5:11).

Increased wealth increases taxation and has the uncanny ability of disappearing right before the eyes of its owners. We are made to wonder if the possession of wealth is worth the effort after all.

• *Why does the possession of money disturb our inner peace?* The person who has money appears to be preoccupied with obtaining more. As a result of his desire, he loses what he really wants – peace and security. "The sleep of the working man is pleasant, whether he eats little or much. But the full stomach of the rich man does not allow him to sleep" (Ecclesiastes 5:12).

In this passage, the Preacher presents two options. The first option is the contentment of the workingman who obviously is not consumed with material gain. He may lack some of the necessities of life or even possess very little of life's essentials. However, he sleeps well at night. The second option is the man who has everything, but along with his surplus he has insomnia. Which option is preferred? Could it not be acceptable to have both? That is the rub, according to the Preacher. We cannot have both.

• *Why does the loss of money seem to follow the surplus of money?* Our desire for material things carries with it a high cost:

> There is a grievous evil which I have seen under the sun: riches being hoarded by their owner to his hurt. When those riches were lost through a bad investment and he had fa-

thered a son, then there was nothing to support him. As he had come naked from his mother's womb, so will he return as he came. He will take nothing from the fruit of his labor that he can carry in his hand. And this also is a grievous evil – exactly as a man is born, thus will he die. So, what is the advantage to him who toils for the wind? Throughout his life he also eats in darkness with great vexation, sickness and anger. (Ecclesiastes 5:13-16)

The Preacher identifies a number of consequences directly linked to material pursuits.

• *First, the wealth seeker can be injured.* Those who seek material gain can be injured by bad investments or by irrational decisions. The desire for financial gain can ruin financial stability. We cannot anticipate what may impact our lives in the future. Taking unnecessary financial risks also puts at risk our ability to meet the needs of our families.

• *Second, the wealth seeker is eventually stripped of his identity.* When we attach our worth to something other than God, we become worthless when that thing is removed. A person leaves this world as he came into it – empty-handed.

• *Finally, the wealth seeker suffers many ills in life.* "Darkness" symbolizes misery. "Vexation" represents the cares and frustrations of life. "Sickness" denotes the physical strain placed upon the body and mind. "Anger" refers to the rage felt when material schemes fail. These consequences show how human opulence is not at all a desirable goal in life.

HUMAN OPPRESSION

The Preacher also is grieved by how human beings treat one another. He admits humans were created good, but they seek many evils. In many areas of life, vices have overtaken any semblance of virtue.

The Preacher observes how wicked and evil men have corrupted the judicial system: "Furthermore, I have seen under the sun that in the place of justice there is wickedness, and in the place of righteousness there is wickedness" (Ecclesiastes 3:16).

The Preacher does not identify any event specifically although we could be confident he has several in mind. The general nature of

Ecclesiastes 3:16 indicates the pervasiveness of corruption. The judicial system should be the bastion of hope for the defenseless and innocent. If those who judge are corrupt, the system fails to fulfill its purpose and therefore becomes a mechanism for evil.

How can the disadvantaged obtain help and receive justice when the courts that should support them are themselves oppressive? "Then I looked again at all the acts of oppression which were being done under the sun. And behold I saw the tears of the oppressed and that they had no one to comfort them; and on the side of their oppressors was power, but they had no one to comfort them" (Ecclesiastes 4:1-2).

In addition to the corrupt judicial system, the Preacher has in mind oppressors in general, referring to anyone who might be over another – king, official or judge. Those who oppress others abuse their power. The Preacher clearly shows the anguish of the oppressed. Their tears are shed without the comfort of a sympathizer. They have no advocate. No one sees nor understands their distress. They suffer alone.

Several passages in both the wisdom literature and the prophets also describe the anguish of those whose cries fall upon deaf ears and then quickly vanish in the cold and cruel air. " 'Because of the devastation of the afflicted, because of the groaning of the needy, Now I will arise,' says the Lord; 'I will set him in the safety for which he longs'" (Psalm 12:5). "Because of the multitude of oppressions they cry out; They cry for help because of the arm of the mighty" (Job 35:9). "For the vineyard of the Lord of hosts is the house of Israel, And the men of Judah His delightful plant. Thus He looked for justice, but behold, bloodshed; For righteousness, but behold, a cry of distress" (Isaiah 5:7).

Although humans may ignore the cries of the oppressed, their Lord certainly does not. God will hold those in power accountable for their actions. Unfortunately, the oppressed must persevere under great duress until God intervenes. Until such time, people in power will continue to mistreat others. That is how the political and judicial bureaucracy works under the sun: "If you see oppression of the poor and denial of justice and righteousness in the province, do not be shocked at the sight, for one official watches over another official, and there are higher officials over them (Ecclesiastes 5:8).

The Preacher has been forthright in his attack against human pride, human opulence and human oppression. These issues generate an air of hopelessness. Why would someone place so much stock in youthful vigor, wealth and dominance? Then again, according to the Preacher, life does not make a lot of sense. But that is how humans behave when they are separated from God.

QUESTIONS FOR PERSONAL AND GROUP REFLECTION

1. How does the Preacher view the subject of youthfulness? How is this view different from that of our present culture?

2. List and discuss the stages of life through which we all pass.

3. How did the Preacher's discussion of human opulence impact you? Do you agree or disagree with his treatment of the subject? Why?

4. What grieves the Preacher about how people treat one another?

5. In what way do the defenseless and the oppressed have hope? How do they find comfort and justice?

11

SEEKING GUIDANCE, FINDING TRUTH

The truth is found when men are free to pursue it.
– Franklin D. Roosevelt (1936)

Guard your steps as you go to the house of God, and draw near
to listen rather than to offer the sacrifice of fools; for they do
not know they are doing evil. (Ecclesiastes 5:1)

"Another day in paradise." That's a phrase my workout buddies and I use to refer to our habitual sweat sessions at the gym. It's a statement that empathetically means, "I feel your pain!"

Pain (and a sudden gripping fear), indeed, is what I felt at one workout session. After a two-week hiatus from my regular workouts during the Christmas holidays, I headed back to "paradise" to begin the new year renewed and invigorated.

My favorite exercise is the bench press. After a few warm-up sets, I began to stack on the weight. I ended the year strong, and I was determined to begin the new year even stronger. I added some weight. And then I added some more. I looked at the bar and thought, "I should be able to add two and half more pounds to each side," so I slapped them on – the more the merrier!

It was time for the magical moment. I sat down, clapped my hands together, grunted a few times, and got myself fired up to pump some iron. I grabbed the bar, brought it down to my chest, and began to push it back up again. The bar didn't budge. I took a deep breath and tried again. Again, the bar didn't move, but gradually got lower until it was touching my chest. I was in trouble. My eyes scanned the gym to see if I could get someone's attention to help me. The bar was now resting on my chest, and I tried to call out to someone, but nothing was coming out of my mouth. It took every bit of my strength to keep the weight from crushing me. "Heeeelp!" I wheezed. To my good fortune, someone reached me in time and helped lift the weight off my chest and placed the heavy bar back into its secure position.

I was humiliated. I thought I could lift all that weight because I had done it before. Of course, I hadn't worked out in two weeks. I learned a very important lesson that day: Use a spotter when you're lifting heavy weights. A spotter is someone who assists us and is there to help if we get into trouble. A spotter can encourage us and motivate us to do more than we think possible. And when we are unable to lift a certain weight because we've grown exhausted, a spotter can aid us as he or she provides that little lift to get us past a sticking point. I should have used a spotter. I was lucky I didn't seriously injure myself.

How many times do we find ourselves needing a spiritual spotter? What a difference it would make to have someone to assist, guide and provide that gentle lift when the weight of the world seems too much to bear alone! Fortunately, we do have an advocate in our corner – someone to strengthen, encourage and motivate us. Whenever we are in need, we should come bravely before the throne of our merciful God. There we will be treated with undeserved kindness and will find the help we need (Hebrews 4:14-16).

Many instructional sections in Ecclesiastes can help us during times of uncertainty and stress. These instructional sections represent the wisdom God has given to humanity to assist, guide and provide a gentle lift. The irony is that humans often reject truths that might help them face the trials of life. The major wisdom sections can be consolidated under four general headings: religion, reality, residency and responsibility.

RELIGION

Religious faith is important to the Preacher. His inspired work is an attempt to lead readers to faithful service to God. Although the Preacher has debated with traditional religious thought, his reverence for God and his thoughts about how to approach God are seen midway in the book. The Preacher warns against a lighthearted approach in our relationship with God. For him, the religion of God is serious business.

According to the Preacher, we should use extreme caution when engaging in certain religious activities.

• *We should be cautious about the praise we offer to God.* "Guard your steps as you go to the house of God, and draw near to listen rather than to offer the sacrifice of fools; for they do not know they are doing evil" (Ecclesiastes 5:1).

The "house of God" probably refers to Solomon's temple built in the 10th century B.C. and destroyed by the Babylonians in 586/7 B.C. The word "house," however, could refer to any place where people approach God in worship (Genesis 28:17, 22; Exodus 23:19; Judges 18:31). "Guard your steps" refers to our demeanor when approaching God. It describes a state of preparedness. The Preacher explains that people should approach God to "listen"; that is, they should be ready to obey God's will. In contrast to such reverence is the "sacrifice of fools." Although they are participants in religious activities, their acts of praise are defined as "doing evil."

King Saul was once called by God to lead an attack against the Amalekites, who opposed Israel when they came up out of Egyptian bondage. God told Joshua on that occasion that the evil Amalekites would one day be destroyed. Now was the time. Samuel gave Saul God's orders – go and utterly destroy them (1 Samuel 15:1-3). Saul led the attack, killing everything but the king and the best of the flock. When the prophet Samuel asked why Saul had not obeyed the Lord, Saul excused his actions by saying how the best of the flock had been spared to offer as sacrifices to God. Samuel condemned Saul's disobedience and said: "Has the Lord as much delight in burn offerings and sacrifices As in obeying the voice of the Lord? Behold, to obey is better than sacrifice, And to heed than the fat of rams" (1 Samuel 15:22).

Saul did not use caution when approaching God in worship. The Preacher would consider Saul's actions as the sacrifice of a fool.

• *We should be cautious when addressing God in prayer.* Prayer is a profound religious act, suitable only for people who revere God: "Do not be hasty in word or impulsive in thought to bring up a matter in the presence of God. For God is in heaven and you are on the earth; therefore let your words be few. For the dream comes through much effort, and the voice of a fool through many words" (Ecclesiastes 5:2-3).

The Preacher is cautioning against thoughtless prayers. God is interested in the content of prayer; He is unimpressed with the mechanics of it. Jesus preached against this same issue when He condemned the hypocrisy of the Pharisees and the pagan rituals of the Gentiles.

> And when you pray, you are not to be as the hypocrites; for they love to stand and pray in the synagogues and on the street corners, in order to be seen by man. ... And when you are praying, do not use meaningless repetition, as the Gentiles do, for they suppose that they will be heard for their many words. (Matthew 6:5, 7)

• *We should be cautious when making promises to God.* The Preacher believes promises made to God should be few and thought through before their utterance:

> When you make a vow to God, do not be late in paying it, for He takes no delight in fools. Pay what you vow! It is better that you should not vow than that you should vow and not pay. Do not let your speech cause you to sin and do not say in the presence of the messenger of God that it was a mistake. Why should God be angry on account of your voice and destroy the work of your hands? For in many dreams and in many words there is emptiness. Rather, fear God. (Ecclesiastes 5:4-7)

A vow is a promise made to God. If we make a promise to God, He will hold us accountable for keeping it. The fool is the one who makes hasty promises without any real intention of keeping them. Perhaps the vow of a fool is really a way in which he attempts to bribe God. Whatever the motive for making a promise, it is sinful not to keep it. In fact, not fulfilling a promise arouses the anger of God. The fear of God leads us to follow through with what we promise.

REALITY

Trials are a part of everyday life. The Preacher approaches the subject of trials in a section where he has brought together in a structured form a number of proverbs and wisdom sayings relating to the trials of life. According to the Preacher, he observes in the world six points of interest regarding trials.

• *Trials are a natural part of life.* This being true, the Preacher believes we should, therefore, learn from the trials of life.

> A good name is better than a good ointment,
> And the day of one's death is better than the day of one's
>   birth.
> It is better to go to a house of mourning
> Than to go to a house of feasting,
> Because that is the end of every man,
> And the living takes it to heart.
> Sorrow is better than laughter,
> For when a face is sad a heart may be happy.
> The mind of the wise is in the house of mourning,
> While the mind of fools is in the house of pleasure.
> It is better to listen to the rebuke of a wise man
> Than for one to listen to the song of fools.
> For as the crackling of thorn bushes under a pot,
> So is the laughter of the fool,
> And this too is futility. (Ecclesiastes 7:1-6)

The reason the day of death is preferred over birth is because it marks an end to the trials and futility of life. A "house of mourning" refers to a funeral or home where someone has died and provides a vivid reminder that our end is getting nearer. A festive occasion does not provide a time for reflection. The same is true of laughter. The Preacher is not interested in the superficiality of good-smelling perfume, festive occasions and laughter. These things offer no insight about human purpose. However, the trials of life can be wonderful opportunities to gain insight into the meaning of human existence.

• *Trials exert pressure upon the human spirit.* Trials can often pressure people to behave in a way inconsistent with the good name they have. Our inner character is always at risk of exposure during trials: "For oppression makes a wise man mad, And a bribe corrupts the heart" (Ecclesiastes 7:7). A wise man may become irrational or "mad," and a wise man, during stressful times, may compromise his character and accept bribes. Consequently, the trials of life can potentially bring us to spiritual ruin.

• *Trials of life offer opportunities for positive outcomes.* The Preacher seeks to help us through the trials of life by helping us look toward a favorable outcome: "The end of a matter is better than its beginning; Patience of spirit is better than haughtiness of spirit" (Ecclesiastes 7:8). Patient endurance under trial will help the sufferer to emerge eventually from the experience. The outcome is what we ultimately make of it.

• *Trials demand that we adjust our attitudes toward them.* Impatience and inappropriate behavior during trials are foolish. "Do not be eager in your heart to be angry, For anger resides in the bosom of fools" (Ecclesiastes 7:9).

The attitude we maintain during difficult times can be the difference between despair and joy. The phrase "eager in your heart" describes the exact opposite of patience. If we possess such a mind, we will buckle under the pressures of life.

• *Trials of life must be faced.* People will inevitably experience times of troubles during their lifetime. When faced with problems, we must not try to avoid them or deny they exist: "Do not say, 'Why is it that the former days were better than these?' For it is not from wisdom that you ask about this" (Ecclesiastes 7:10).

Humans make the common mistake of imagining the former days were the best. Upon closer scrutiny, however, the former days had their fair share of problems as well. Time has simply erased some of the memories of those troublesome days. The Preacher says it is unwise to relive the past while making no progress in the present.

• *Trials test the resiliency of the human spirit.* The resilient are those who are wise to the trials of life and have a relenting spirit of optimism in God. Wisdom is the key to human resilience. "Wisdom along with an inheritance is good And an advantage to those who see the sun. For wisdom is protection just as money is protection. But the advantage of knowledge is that wisdom preserves the lives of its possessors" (7:11-12).

This wisdom grows out of faith (Ecclesiastes 7:13), provides stability during good and bad times (v. 14), and helps us be honest enough to admit our need for help (vv. 19-22).

RESIDENCY

The Preacher has much to say about the proper attitude and behavior of citizens toward people in authority. Respect for and lack of respect for leaders are indicators of a strong or weak moral character, respectively.

> I say, "Keep the command of the king because of the oath before God. Do not be in a hurry to leave him. Do not join in an evil matter, for he will do whatever he pleases." Since the word of the king is authoritative, who will say to him, "What are you doing?" He who keeps a royal command experiences no trouble, for a wise heart knows the proper time and procedure. (Ecclesiastes 8:2-5)

The Preacher offers the following observations for people who have the good sense to be model citizens:

• *Understand government is divinely appointed.* God approves the existence of governing bodies and authorities (Ecclesiastes 8:2; cf. Romans 13:1-7). God is opposed to any government that corrupts justice. Kings and all heads of authority are accountable to God.

• *Good citizens are to shore up their leaders* (Ecclesiastes 8:3-4; 10:20; cf. 1 Thessalonians 5:12). That is to say, it is wiser to be loyal to leaders than to rebel against their leadership.

• *Good citizens will submit to their leaders* (Ecclesiastes 8:5a; cf. Hebrews 13:7, 17). Respectful and obedient people have nothing to fear from their government.

• *Good citizens show good judgment toward leaders* (Ecclesiastes 8:5b; cf. 1 Timothy 5:19). Leaders have authority and power over the people they govern – power for good and evil. It makes sense that we show candor and knowledge of the way things work when dealing with leaders in the government. As the Preacher says, there is a "proper time and procedure" when approaching governmental leaders about a matter. This would, of course, indicate that there are improper times and procedures.

RESPONSIBILITY

The Preacher is a champion of human responsibility. We could get the impression while reading Ecclesiastes that if human toil is fruitless, why not depend upon others for our survival? Nothing, however, could be further from the truth. Toiling in the context of a world without God is fruitless. In other words, God breathes meaning into life when we fear Him – life takes on a completely different meaning. People now have a purpose to their existence that inspires their endeavors. Living successfully under God's will requires knowledge of how God has arranged the laws and principles of the world. When we believe these principles and abide by them, our labor will be joyous.

• *The first law of human effectiveness revolves around an enduring principle – we reap what we sow.* The Preacher states the matter in a figurative way: "Cast your bread on the surface of the waters, for you will find it after many days (Ecclesiastes 11:1).

To "cast" is to take a venture of faith. "Bread" refers to our livelihood. In essence, the Preacher is encouraging us to step out on faith and commit ourselves to the task of providing a living. The phrase "after many days" describes patient diligence knowing rewards will come although we may not know exactly when. Life should be taken from the "hand of God" despite all the trials, frustrations and perplexities. One day, as the Preacher says, "you will find it."

• *The second law of human effectiveness calls for us to insulate against the misfortunes of life.* The Preacher teaches repeatedly how life is full of surprises. To counter the elements of time and chance, we should not have all our eggs in one basket.

> Divide your portion to seven, or even to eight, for you do
> not know what misfortune may occur on the earth. If the
> clouds are full, they pour out rain upon the earth; and whether
> a tree falls toward the south or toward the north, wherever
> the tree falls, there it lies. (Ecclesiastes 11:2-3)

The reference to the fallen tree may refer to the sudden misfortunes of life. The tree was uprooted by an unpredictable act of nature. Where the tree falls, there – in that place – it becomes an obstacle; yet, people are to continue their work on earth by removing the tree (or obstacle) from where it lies.

• *The third law of human effectiveness is that we should increase the odds of success.* The unpredictable nature of the world should not cause hesitation in our work. He who watches for a perfect condition before he acts will wait an eternity. There are no perfect conditions. We must consistently work despite unfavorable conditions.

> He who watches the wind will not sow and he who looks at the clouds will not reap. Just as you do not know the path of the wind and how bones are formed in the womb of the pregnant woman, so you do not know the activity of God who makes all things. Sow your seed in the morning, and do not be idle in the evening, for you do not know whether morning or evening sowing will succeed, or whether both of them alike will be good. (Ecclesiastes 11:4-6)

Although we live in an uncertain and unpredictable world, some things do make sense. God's instructional or wisdom material in Ecclesiastes serves as a spiritual spotter to help lift the weight of our trials, turmoil and temptations.

QUESTIONS FOR PERSONAL AND GROUP REFLECTION

1. What can you learn about the Preacher's faith from his comments about religion? Do you consider him to be an apostate, orthodox or somewhere in between?

2. Do you believe the Preacher's comments about religion are helpful? Find similar thoughts in the New Testament that relate to the concerns of the Preacher.

3. Which points of interest regarding trials do you find the most helpful? Do you believe the Preacher's observations are valid? Explain.

4. Why do you think the Preacher addresses the issue of proper attitude toward the government? Why would this be a pressing concern for him?

5. Discuss how the laws of human effectiveness relate to the world today?

12

SEEKING HONESTY, FINDING HOPE

Lord, through this hour Be Thou our Guide
So by Thy power No foot shall slide.
– Westminster Chimes

The words of wise men are like goads,
and masters of these collections are like well-driven nails;
they are given by one Shepherd. (Ecclesiastes 12:11)

After reading Ecclesiastes, we could easily assume the Preacher couldn't find one honest person who would be truthful about the enigmas of life and religion. Most people would assert the Preacher had a pessimistic view of life. He says very little inspiring optimism. The Preacher has concluded life is vanity. However, such an interpretation of the Preacher's view is actually a distortion. The Preacher was pessimistic about a life without God, and he was certainly a realist when it came to a life with God. In his realism, the Preacher revealed his optimism.

THE LANGUAGE OF A PESSIMIST

We detect the pessimism of the Preacher by observing specific words he uses to convey his message. These words indicate how the Preacher feels and how he perceives life under the sun. The Preacher sets a pessimistic tone for Ecclesiastes when he draws upon a number of key words conveying his frustrated feelings about life. The most frequent word the Preacher uses to express his pessimism is "vanity." The word "vanity" is used more than 30 times to summarize human activity under the sun. Because of the Preacher's literary technique (Ecclesiastes 1:2; 12:8), the message of the book of Ecclesiastes is the theme of vanity. Everything, according to the Preacher, comes under the umbrella of vanity – life and death and everything in between.

The Preacher uses the words "trouble," "evil thing" or "laboring" to express what we face in the world. These words convey the idea of laborious toil, distress, disaster and misfortune. These ideas represent the trouble or evil we may find in the world. Human labor is troublesome. "Thus I hated all the fruit of my labor for which I had labored under the sun, for I must leave it to the man who will come after me" (Ecclesiastes 2:18).

Another frequently used term is "evil." This word refers to misery, trouble and disaster. The Preacher, on occasion, will apply this term by referring to evil as a grievous evil: "There is a grievous evil which I have seen under the sun: riches being hoarded by their owner to his hurt" (Ecclesiastes 5:13).

"Death" and "dying" are favorite terms used in Ecclesiastes. The Preacher's obsession with these terms accentuates the pessimistic tone of his message. Ecclesiastes 3:19 is a classic example of the Preacher's cynicism and pessimism about life: "For the fate of the sons of men and the fate of beasts is the same. As one dies so dies the other; indeed, they all have the same breath and there is no advantage for man over beast, for all is vanity."

In fact, the Preacher recommends death over life if it is true that all human activity is vanity anyhow. "So I congratulated the dead who are already dead more than the living who are still living" (Ecclesiastes 4:2).

Adding to the pessimism of the book is the notion that the Preacher is hedged in by wrongdoing or wickedness. The Preacher refers to the behavior and activity of the wicked 12 times. Wickedness overruns righteousness, and those who do wrong outnumber those who try to do right. According to the Preacher, the world is completely turned upside down.

> There is futility which is done on the earth, that is, there are righteous men to whom it happens according to the deeds of the wicked. On the other hand, there are evil men to whom it happens according to the deeds of the righteous. I say that this too is futility. (Ecclesiastes 8:14)

The final term of interest is the word translated "vexation" or "sorrow." This word appears seven times and describes the irritation, distress and burdens that life under the sun imposes upon the living. For example, those who labor in vanity should contemplate whether their fruitless labor is worth the impact that such activity will have upon them physically and mentally. "Throughout his life he also eats in darkness with great vexation, sickness and anger" (Ecclesiastes 5:17).

Because of all the negative things the Preacher observes, it is understandable why he fell into a state of despair (Ecclesiastes 2:20). He repeatedly says he hates life (vv. 17-18) because everything surrounding him causes him much grief (vv. 17, 23). Is the Preacher a hopeless case? Can we find anything of value in his message? Before we judge too harshly the pessimistic tone of the Preacher, we need to keep in mind that the Preacher's pessimism is based from the perspective that a life without God serves no useful purpose.

THE LESSONS OF A REALIST

Although the Preacher appears to be a pessimist, he is really more of a realist. His realism is based upon what he has experienced and observed about life. His message is not devoid of any optimism or hope. However, his aim is to be frank about the life a person may choose to live without God. His approach might be comparable to a parent taking his or her young teenager down to skid row to teach the youngster about the despair and demoralizing way of life characterizing people who abuse alcohol, drugs and sex. The scene of such human emptiness is real and horrifying and could have a profound impression upon a young mind.

We may wonder, however, why we should trust what the Preacher says about a life without God. As the Preacher closes out his message, he reminds us of his credibility and trustworthiness.

> In addition to being a wise man, the Preacher also taught the people knowledge; and he pondered, searched out and arranged many proverbs. The Preacher sought to find delightful words and to write words of truth correctly. The words of wise men are like goads, and masters of these collections are like well-driven nails; they are given by one Shepherd. But beyond this, my son, be warned: the writing of many books is endless, and excessive devotion to books

is wearying to the body. The conclusion, when all has been heard, is: fear God and keep His commandments, because this applies to every person. For God will bring every act to judgment, everything which is hidden, whether it is good or evil. (Ecclesiastes 12:9-14)

Is the Preacher worthy of our confidence? He offers himself as a credible witness of the world under the sun because he has drawn upon the experiences of others – such as King Solomon – and compared these experiences to his own. The Preacher describes himself as a wise preacher or teacher and gives several reasons as to why his testimony is trustworthy.

• *First, the Preacher's words are trustworthy because he has followed the path of wisdom.* The Preacher seems to imply that he is a part of a class of people devoted to teaching others about the wisdom of God. One of the indications of such a special recognition is the Preacher's objective to teach people to "fear God." Wise men were known for teaching the fear of the Lord (Deuteronomy 6:1-9).

The Preacher, like Moses, Solomon (Proverbs 1:7), and Ezra the priest (Ezra 7:10), used his wisdom and knowledge to teach other people to fear the Lord.

• *Second, the Preacher's words are trustworthy because he has personally experienced the emptiness of worldly pursuits.* The Preacher is truly a mentor, someone who can encourage and offer personal guidance. According to Ecclesiastes 12:9, the Preacher has "knowledge" about life. This knowledge means more than the accumulation of facts. Knowledge implies sufficient life experience to make accurate judgments. Consequently, the Preacher's method of instruction is more pastoral than the dissemination of facts. This is consistent with the teaching methods of wise men. Often in biblical literature, teachers are pictured as fathers or mothers and their pupils as sons or children.

• *Third, the Preacher's words are trustworthy because he has thoroughly investigated the alternative to fearing God.* According to Ecclesiastes 12:9, we can trust the Preacher. He "pondered" the way of the world. This word means he weighed and evaluated what he observed and experienced in the world and compared it to the life God gives. When the evaluations were completed, there was but one conclusion – "fear God and keep His commandments." His conclusion was based upon a complete and diligent investigation. The text says he "searched out." In other words, no stone was left unturned. Everything passed under the microscope, and even the smallest details were scrutinized intensively. The Preacher skillfully arranged his findings. The arrangement refers to the orderliness of his presentation.

• *Fourth, the Preacher's words are trustworthy because they are the words of God.* God is symbolized as the "one Shepherd." In the wisdom tradition, the shepherd image is often applied to the manner in which God interacts and leads His people (Psalm 23; Ezekiel 34:1-10). According to Ecclesiastes 12:11-14, the words of the Shepherd are, first of all, instructional. They are like "goads" and "well-driven nails." These images mean the word of God prods human behavior as well as penetrates the human heart. The gifts of God are many in Ecclesiastes. Some of these gifts, like the task of dealing with life, may not be so pleasant; other gifts, like the gift of joy in labor, are more palatable. The message of the Preacher contained in Ecclesiastes is also a gift from God. Humans are fortunate to have such a detailed evaluation of what life is like without God. People who may take their relationship with God for granted would do well to read the Preacher's words again and again.

• *Finally, the words of the Shepherd are sufficient.* The Preacher issues a warning about the reading of uninspired material: "But beyond this, my son, be warned: the writing of many books is endless, and excessive devotion to books is wearying to the body" (Ecclesiastes 12:12).

Beyond the words of God, we must exercise caution. An endless number of books can occupy our time. A student of wisdom should make it his priority to devour the words from the Shepherd and evaluate other books by the Shepherd's wisdom. Paul acknowledged the adequacy of inspired scripture to provide all that is needed to equip us for serving God: "All scripture is inspired by God and profitable for teaching, for reproof, for correction, for training in righteousness; that the man of God may be adequate, equipped for every good work" (2 Timothy 3:16-17).

When the devil tempted Jesus to turn stones to bread, Jesus countered the temptations by affirming the sufficiency of God's Word to provide everything He ultimately needed. "It is written, 'Man shall not live on bread alone, but on every word that proceeds out of the mouth of God'" (Matthew 4:4).

The words of the Shepherd are also words leading to salvation. The reason the Word of God is so important is because it prepares people for their appointment with God. "The conclusion, when all has been heard, is: fear God and keep His commandments, because this applies to every person. For God will bring every act to judgment, everything which is hidden, whether it is good or bad" (Ecclesiastes 12:13-14).

The Preacher has mentioned in several key places that God will hold us accountable for our actions. "I said to myself, 'God will judge both the righteous man and the wicked man,' for a time for every matter and for every deed there is" (Ecclesiastes 3:17). "Rejoice, young man, during your childhood, and let your heart be pleasant during the days of young manhood. And follow the impulses of your heart and the desires of your eyes. Yet know that God will bring you to judgment for all these things" (11:9).

Based upon the judgment to come, the Preacher closes his message with three very important truths about preparing ourselves to meet God (and Christ – John 5:27; Revelation 20:11-13) in judgment. First, we should develop the right attitude toward God – "fear" or reverential awe. Second, we should guard our actions – "keep His commandments." And finally, we should keep our heart pure – that which is "hidden" will be exposed.

Is there hope for a pessimist? The Preacher believes there is. That is why he is forthright in his observation about the world. Pessimism is the natural consequence of life under the sun; optimism is the natural consequence of fearing God. In fact, the Preacher was so optimistic about the life of those who fear the Lord that he wrote to inform his readers about the tragedy of the alternative.

QUESTIONS FOR PERSONAL AND GROUP REFLECTION

1. Why is the book of Ecclesiastes considered to be a pessimistic book? Is this a fair evaluation in light of the contents of the book of Ecclesiastes?

2. Discuss the different words the Preacher employs to stress his view about life without God. What are these words meant to convey?

3. Why are the Preacher's observations about life trustworthy?

4. Does the Preacher appear to be an optimist, a realist or a pessimist?

5. Discuss the impact of the Preacher's concluding thoughts. Do you believe the Preacher has achieved his purpose?

13

SEEKING GOD, FINDING HAPPINESS

O happiness! Our being's end and aim!
Good, pleasure, ease, content! Whate'er thy name.
– Alexander Pope (Essay on Man), 1733-1734

So I commended pleasure, for there is nothing good
for a man under the sun except to eat and to drink
and to be merry. (Ecclesiastes 8:15)

"SEE Jesus" is our motto at the Timberlane Church of Christ and it serves as a theology of life. We have attempted to establish a framework out of which we understand our own identity and how we can effectively relate to the world around us. This motto reminds us what our mission is. We've constructed a mission declaration that keeps us focused as we carry out the work of God in our community. The mission declaration is: "We are dedicated to the growth of God's family. We will seek the lost, embrace them in God's love, and equip them to serve God."

We have committed ourselves as a congregation and as individual Christians to church growth. According to the Great Commission, God's church grows through evangelism and assimilation. Based upon the model of the Great Commission to go and teach (Matthew 28:18-20), we understand God to mean seek, embrace and equip. From these three words we've constructed the acronym, SEE. Because Jesus said the only way to God is through Him (John 14:6), we added Jesus to the acronym, creating our congregational motto – "SEE Jesus." All that we do is connected to this mission.

A theology of life is not a unique idea. Jesus had a theology of life, a framework out of which He understood the world around Him. He summarized it in a succinct way in a conversation He once had with

His disciples when they were questioning Him about what He was going to eat: "My food is to do the will of Him who sent Me, and to accomplish His work" (John 4:34).

Jesus also provided a framework out of which His disciples were to think of themselves. In a prayer He prayed on behalf of His disciples, Jesus said to the Father, "They are not of the world even as I am not of the world" (John 17:16). Jesus wanted His disciples to understand that their values and views concerning how they interacted with the world derived from a heavenly source. Paul offered a similar inspired theology of life for the Christians living in the city of Philippi when he wrote, "For our citizenship is in heaven" (Philippians 3:20).

The Preacher in Ecclesiastes has an intriguing theology of life – one that is subtle and could be overlooked if we don't read his book carefully. The Preacher's theology of life is compelling as well as puzzling – eat, drink and be merry (Ecclesiastes 2:24; 8:15; 9:7).

This statement may surprise some people. Other people may be shocked, even outraged. Before we draw any unwarranted conclusions, we must allow the Preacher to explain himself. The way the Preacher chooses to present his case is just as compelling and puzzling as the Preacher's theology of life statement.

MEANINGS OF VANITY

The author of Ecclesiastes was a preacher par excellence. He identifies himself as a preacher, a teacher of wisdom (Ecclesiastes 1:1, 12; 7:27; 12:8-10). His wisdom is presented in the form of a sermon. According to Ecclesiastes 12:9, the Preacher arranged his material in an orderly manner. Ecclesiastes has all the elements of a sermon – an introduction, a body filled with riveting points and illustrations, and a conclusion.

The problem the Preacher's sermon addresses is the problem of the vanity of life. What does he mean by the "vanity of life"? Does he mean life is not worth living? How are people of faith to understand the words of the Preacher when his message appears to be faith's antagonist? Ironically, the Preacher's vanity theme is not much different from Paul's view of the world in his letter to the Romans where he states the created world was subjected to futility (Romans 8:20). A consistency of the vanity theme is in the Old and New Testaments. To arrive at the precise meaning, we need a quick review of the Preacher's use of the term.

"Vanity of vanities" (Ecclesiastes 1:2; 12:8) is a Hebrew superlative that means "utter vanity!" Vanity comes from the Hebrew word *hebel* and has a wide variety of meanings.

• *Vanity can refer to the brevity, emptiness or the insubstantiality of a person, place or thing.* For instance, As Job reflects upon his life while sitting upon the ash-heap, he laments:

> Remember that my life is but breath,
> My eye will not again see good.
> The eye of him who sees me will behold me no more;
> Thine eyes will be on me, but I will not be.
> When a cloud vanishes, it is gone,
> So he who goes down to Sheol does not come up.
> He will not return again to his house,
> Nor will his place know him anymore.
> Therefore, I will not restrain my mouth;
> I will speak in the anguish of my spirit,
> I will complain in the bitterness of my soul.
> Am I the sea, or the sea monster,
> That Thou dost set a guard over me?
> If I say, "My bed will comfort me,
> My couch will ease my complaint,"
> Then Thou dost frighten me with dreams
> And terrify me by visions;
> So that my soul would choose suffocation,
> Death rather than my pains.
> I waste away; I will not live forever.
> Leave me alone, for my days are but a breath.
> (Job 7:7-16)

The vanity of Job's life is clear. He acknowledges the brevity of his life and compares it to his own breath. He feels nothing but emptiness as he is wasting away. Job believes his life is unsubstantial and inconsequential to anything else. Job could not be more vivid in describing the vanity of life from a personal point of view.

• *Vanity may refer to something that is unreliable or frail.* The psalmist cautions people of faith about trusting in unscrupulous people:

> Men of low degree are only vanity, and men of rank are a lie; In the balances they go up; They are together lighter than breath. Do not trust in oppression, And do not vainly hope in robbery; If riches increase, do not set your heart upon them. (Psalm 62:9-10)

• *Vanity can be connected to futility.* As Job's comforters try to get him to acknowledge sins he knows he has not committed, he pleads for a mediator. Job feels an injustice had been committed against him. He accuses God of not playing fairly. Job reasons that one should be innocent until proven guilty; yet, God had already judged him to be guilty. Consequently, why should Job try to prove his innocence? "I am accounted wicked, Why then should I toil in vain?" (Job 9:29).

Job considered his efforts as an exercise in futility. There was no purpose to his life, no hope.

• *Vanity can refer to what is deceitful.* Because of the idolatry of the Israelites, God tells Jeremiah He is going to punish them, and doubly repay their iniquity. Jeremiah is concerned about God's retribution and reputation. He is afraid the nations will accuse God of being deceitful with His people after He has promised to do them good: "O Lord, my strength and my stronghold, And my refuge in the day of distress,To Thee the nations will come From the ends of the earth And say, 'Our fathers have inherited nothing but falsehood, Futility and things of no profit'" (Jeremiah 16:19).

HOW THE PREACHER SEES VANITY

All four of these meanings of vanity are found in Ecclesiastes. The Preacher attaches vanity, futility, emptiness, unreliability and deceit to an array of human experience.

• *The Preacher finds vanity in all human activity.* "I have seen all the works which have been done under the sun, and behold, all is vanity and striving after wind" (Ecclesiastes 1:14). After summarizing life in general, the Preacher focuses upon the vanity in other facets of life.

• *The Preacher sees only vanity in what people refer to as joy.* "I said to myself, 'Come now, I will test you with pleasure. So enjoy yourself.'

And behold, it too was futility" (Ecclesiastes 2:1).

• *The Preacher observes how frustrating life can be for people who never seem to be satisfied by the fruits of their labor.*

> And I have seen that every labor and every skill which is done is the result of rivalry between a man and his neighbor. This too is vanity and striving after wind. ... Then I looked again at vanity under the sun. There was a certain man without a dependent, having neither a son nor a brother, yet there was no end to all his labor. Indeed, his eyes were not satisfied with riches and he never asked, "And for whom am I laboring and depriving myself of pleasure?" This too is vanity and it is a grievous task. ... He who loves money will not be satisfied with money, nor he who loves abundance with its income. This too is vanity. (Ecclesiastes 4:4, 7-8; 5:10)

• *The Preacher believes life itself is subject to vanity.* "So I hated life, for the work which had been done under the sun was grievous to me; because everything is futility and striving after wind" (Ecclesiastes 2:17).

The Preacher concludes there is no real difference between the diligent and the idle, for they both have the same destiny. "For what does a man get in all his labor and in his striving with which he labors under the sun?" (Ecclesiastes 2:22).

In a similar fashion, he also admits the destinies of the wise and the foolish are the same: "Then I said to myself, 'As is the fate of the fool, it will also befall me. Why then have I been extremely wise?'" (Ecclesiastes 2:15).

The Preacher sees no real advantage people have over animals in death. "For the fate of the sons of men and the fate of beasts is the same. As one dies so dies the other; indeed, they all have the same breath and there is no advantage for man over beast, for all is vanity" (Ecclesiastes 3:19).

Why does he view life in such a pessimistic way? Think for just a moment how the New Testament views life. Remember when Paul said the created world is subject to futility? He also stated that when we are alive we are at the same time wasting away (2 Corinthians 4:16). Ironically, while a person knows this is happening (v. 8), he still expects, hopes and waits for something different (Romans 8:25). Life through the lens of the New Testament is also an enigma.

What does the Preacher mean by referring to life as vanity? Is all of life subject to futility? Or is there a dimension of life the Preacher deems as futility? The Preacher sees the believer living in an overlap (Eaton 57). On the one hand, life is devoid of any spiritual dimension. All activities, human desires and social engagements from this perspective are futile. On the other hand, life is filled with faith.

Although somewhat masked at first, the Preacher's attachment to the spiritual begins to build in momentum until he reaches his climactic conclusion that the whole duty of man is to fear God and keep His commandments. Obviously, the Preacher does not think his concluding statement is vanity of vanities! Remember, Jesus once said to His disciples that they were in the world but not of the world (John 17:14).

Living life from a faith perspective may bring true purpose and meaning. It does not necessarily solve all the enigmas, mysteries or the injustices of life. This is precisely what the Preacher wants us to understand. Then how do people of faith live? How do they interpret the apparent contradictions of life? His answer is surprising and couched in language easily misunderstood.

EAT, DRINK AND BE MERRY

Alongside the Preacher's theme of vanity is the second theme: Eat, drink and be merry. The Preacher uses the proverbial form "there is nothing better," and then writes how our highest achievement in this life is to eat, drink and be merry. "There is nothing better for a man than to eat and drink and tell himself that his labor is good" (Ecclesiastes 2:24). "I know that there is nothing better for them than to rejoice and to do good in one's lifetime; moreover, that every man who eats and drinks sees good in all his labor" (3:12). "And I have seen that nothing is better than that man should be happy in his activities, for that is his lot" (v. 22). "So I commended pleasure, for there is nothing good for a man under the sun except to eat and to drink and to be merry" (8:15; cf. 9:7-9).

The advice of the Preacher sounds much like something from pagan philosophy. Is he encouraging people of faith to follow a hedonistic lifestyle? The Epicureans are credited with the slogan "eat, drink and be merry." Epicurus was born in 341 B.C. and died in 270 B.C. He was one of the most influential of the Greek philosophers. His popularity attracted not only loyal followers, but he also was one of the most controversial figures in ancient philosophy. Many of Epicurus' disciples lived on his property in order to withdraw from society. Such exclusion invited public scrutiny and unpopularity. Epicurus admittedly allowed women, courtesans and slaves into his private community. This action, along with his professed hedonism, became the source of much gossip and circulating tales about his school and teachings.

Epicureanism had degenerated into mere materialism at the time of the first century, but such was not the case initially. Epicurus and his disciples devoted themselves primarily to the pursuit of personal, individual happiness in contrast to other philosophers who emphasized virtue. The highest attainment for Epicurus was the absence of pain. Because Epicurus did not believe in life after death, he rejected any notion of a divine retribution. In his mind, the gods did not care for human life. Consequently, the motto became "let us eat, drink and be merry, for tomorrow we die!"

In some instances the Preacher does sound a bit Epicurean. The most obvious connection is his eat, drink and be merry motif. However, it must be borne in mind that Epicureanism came nearly 600 years after the Preacher. Epicureanism emphasized the enjoyment of life with an emphasis upon the here and now; the Preacher, however, emphasized the enjoyment of life in view of the hereafter. Consequently, the virtue of living responsibly comes into play from the vantage point of the Preacher. According to the Preacher, God does care about human life, and there will also be a day of accountability of human activity: "For God will bring every act to judgment, everything which is hidden, whether it is good or evil" (Ecclesiastes 12:14).

What exactly does the Preacher mean by his phrase "eat, drink and be merry"? We could get the impression that he is encouraging fleshly indulgence, but we might also think he is discouraging fleshly pleasure. From all indications, it appears the Preacher is not advising worldliness because he already refers to such pursuits as vanity. He may be encouraging a state of contentment. The phrase "eating, drinking and rejoicing" is an idiom for being full of life, satisfied, contented. The cultural pursuit of earthly wisdom, wealth, power or pleasure exclusively without any faith commitment to God is what the Preacher describes as "vanity of vanities." He does not mean life itself cannot be enjoyed. A state of contentment is also what the New Testament encourages: "For everything created by God is good, and nothing is to be rejected, if it is received with gratitude" (1 Timothy 4:4). "But godliness actually is a means of great gain, when accompanied by contentment. For we have brought nothing into the world, so we cannot take anything out of it either. And if we have food and covering, with these we shall be content" (6:6-8).

To eat, drink and be merry is the Preacher's way of countering the futility of life without God. After his pessimistic introduction and obvious theme of vanity, the mood changes in Ecclesiastes 2:24-25: "There is nothing better for a man than to eat and drink and tell himself that his labor is good. This also I have seen, that it is from the hand of God. For who can eat and who can have enjoyment without Him?"

The Preacher introduces God, and the vanity of things done under the sun begins to fade slowly in His dominance. Three important confessions of the Preacher form the basis of his theology of contentment and enjoyment of life.

• *The Preacher believes life should be enjoyed.* Life is characterized by uncertainties, adversities and mysteries; nevertheless, humans are to enjoy the world God made for them. They are to make the best of their lives and enjoy their labors and toils. We must come to understand we cannot find and discover all the answers to life's dilemmas, but we can enjoy living despite them. "Here is what I have seen to be good and fitting: to eat, to drink and enjoy oneself in all one's labor in which he toils under the sun during the few years of his life which God has given him; for this is his reward" (Ecclesiastes 5:18).

• *The Preacher believes the capacity to enjoy life is God's gift to us.* Ecclesiastes 2:24 says this gift is "from the hand of God." The Preacher says humanity can have a joyful portion from God (Ecclesiastes 2:10, 21; 3:22; 5:18-19; 9:6, 9). God is concerned about our joy and happiness (2:25; 3:12; 5:18, 20; 9:7; 11:7-9). Consequently, the pursuit of happiness outside of a relationship of faith in Him is futile.

• *As a general rule, when we live to please God, He bestows upon us gifts of wisdom, knowledge and joy.* These three confessions form the basis of the Preacher's highly developed theology of life.

The enjoyment of life in Ecclesiastes eventually overtakes the vanity of life. The enjoyment of life comes about by living in such a way as to please God (Hebrews 11:6) and by receiving God's gifts (James 1:17). There is no solution to futility other than to view the problem in the light of God's purpose for humanity. The only possible means of enjoying life, according to the Preacher, is to live under God's gracious care and sovereignty. "In the day of prosperity be happy, But in the day of adversity consider – God has made the one as well as the other So that man may not discover anything that will be after him (Ecclesiastes 7:14).

ON A MORE PERSONAL NOTE

As I conclude this book, my thoughts turn to Jerry, a Christian man in the congregation where I serve. Honestly, when I think of him, I don't know whether to laugh or cry. Jerry was a witty and unassuming man, short in stature and full of faith. Most of his life was spent going back and forth to doctors and in and out of hospitals. Jerry was born with what is called a blood tumor on his face. The tumor could not be removed at birth because he would have bled to death. The tumor disfigured a little more than half his face. Some people found his looks disturbing. Jerry's beauty, however, was found in his heart. And everyone who knew him was touched by his love, kindness and faith in God.

Jerry's recent prognosis wasn't good. He was dying of cancer, and hospice was with him 24 hours a day. Before he slid into a coma, he called to ask if I would come out to see him. I grabbed Bob, one of the elders of the church, and we drove to his home.

Jerry was feeling pretty well that evening because he had received some pain medication and wanted to use the opportunity to make some final requests about his funeral service. We entered his home, hugged his gracious and loyal wife, Theresa, and sat down opposite Jerry. He was sitting on the couch, feet propped up, and breathing heavily into an oxygen mask. After clearing his throat, covering the hole where he had had a tracheotomy, Jerry began to speak:

"I want to thank you both for coming to see me tonight."

"No problem, it's our pleasure, Jerry. What can we do for you?"

Jerry again cleared his throat and drew a big breath into his lungs and said, "I want you to read Psalm 23 for me."

After I read the psalm, Jerry asked, "Am I going through the 'valley of the shadow of death?'"

"Yes," I responded, and then continued to talk about why Psalm 23 was written and how the psalm pictures God as a wonderful Shepherd who is with us every step of the way – during good times and bad times.

"I'm ready," Jerry said with hope and confidence. Bob and I knelt down beside Jerry, and all of us held hands and prayed. Jerry died shortly thereafter.

Jerry was ready. His faith was the kind of faith the Preacher was talking about in Ecclesiastes. Jerry lived his life eating, drinking and being merry because he feared God. Although his life was cut short, he lived a full life nonetheless. Jerry had the longer view of life. He wasn't solely living for the here and now, but he – by faith – lived in view of an eternal future. Jerry's life was one with purpose – a life of happiness, not dependent upon external circumstances but upon internal trust in a loving Shepherd.

This life God also promises to you. You can have the best of both worlds – a life of purpose now and the anticipation of life in eternity with God later. Life can't get any better than that! "It is good that you grasp one thing, and also not let go of the other; for the one who fears God comes forth with both of them" (Ecclesiastes 7:18).

The only way to achieve true happiness in life is found in serving God. "The conclusion, when all has been heard, is: fear God and keep His commandments, because this applies to every person" (Ecclesiastes 12:13).

QUESTIONS FOR PERSONAL AND GROUP REFLECTION

1. What is a theology of life? What practical purpose does one serve?

2. What is the problem of life the Preacher addresses? How is this problem the antagonist of faith?

3. What are the different meanings of "vanity of vanities"? Where else in Scripture can you find references to the vanity of life?

4. What about life is vanity according to the Preacher?

5. What does the Preacher mean by eat, drink and be merry? How is he different from the Epicureans?

SELECTED
BIBLIOGRAPHY

Ancient Near Eastern Texts (ANET). James B. Pritchard, ed. New Jersey: Princeton UP, 1969, third ed.

Anderson, Bernhard W. *Understanding the Old Testament*. Englewood Cliffs: Prentice-Hall, 1984, fourth ed.

Archer, Gleason L., Jr. *A Survey of Old Testament Introduction*. Chicago: Moody Press, 1974. Revised.

_____. "Ecclesiastes." *The Zondervan Pictorial Encyclopedia of the Bible*, Merrill C. Tenney, gen. ed. Grand Rapids: Zondervan, 1975. II:184-190.

Beecher, W. J. and C. E. Armerding. "Ecclesiastes." *The International Standard Bible Encyclopedia*, Geoffrey W. Bromiley, gen. ed. Grand Rapids: Eerdmans, 1982. II:11-14.

Crenshaw, James L. *Ecclesiastes*. Philadelphia: Westminster, 1987.

_____. "Method in Determining Wisdom Influence upon 'Historical' Literature." *Journal of Biblical Literature* 88 (1969): 129-142.

Davidson, Robert. *Ecclesiastes and the Song of Solomon. The Daily Study Bible Series*. John C.L. Gibson, gen. ed. Philadelphia: Westminster Press, 1986.

Eaton, Michael A. *Ecclesiastes, Tyndale Old Testament Commentaries*. D. J. Wiseman, ed. Downers Grove: Inter-Varsity Press, 1983.

"Ecclesiastes." *The Interpreter's Bible*. Volume V. George Arthur Buttrick, General Editor. Nashville: Abingdon Press, 1956.

Emerton, J. A. "Wisdom." *Tradition and Interpretation*. G. W. Anderson, ed. Oxford: Clarendon, 1979.

"Epicureans." *Smith's Bible Dictionary*. Nashville: Holman Bible Publishers, ND. Revised.

Ferguson, Everett. *Backgrounds of Early Christianity*. Grand Rapids: William B. Eerdmans, 1993, second edition.

Gleaves, G. Scott. "Preachers Are People Too." *Gospel Advocate* (June, 2000): 13-14.

Holladay, William L. *A Concise Hebrew and Aramaic Lexicon of the Old Testament*. Grand Rapids: William B. Eerdmans, 1988.

Josephus, Flavius. *The Works of Flavius Josephus*. William Whiston, Translator. Volume IV. Grand Rapids: Baker Book House, 1974.

McComiskey, Thomas E. "Ecclesiastes." *Baker Encyclopedia of the Bible*. Walter A. Elwell, gen. ed. Grand Rapids: Baker, 1988. I:651-654.

Murphy, Roland E. *Ecclesiastes, Word Biblical Commentary*. David A. Hubbard and Glen W. Barker, gen. eds. Dallas: Word Publishers, 1992.

Murphy, Roland E. and Elizabeth Huwiler. *Proverbs, Ecclesiastes, Song of Solomon. New International Biblical Commentary*. Robert L. Hubbard and Robert K. Johnston, gen. eds. Peabody: Hendrickson Publishers, 1999. XII:170-171.

Nouwen, Henri J.M. *The Way of the Heart: Desert Spirituality and Contemporary Ministry*. New York: Seabury P, 1981.

Rad, Gerhard von. *Wisdom in Israel*. Nashville: Abingdon, 1972.

Rankin, O.S. *Ecclesiastes. The Interpreter's Bible*. George Arthur Buttrick, ed. Nashville: Eerdmans, 1993, second edition. V:4.

Roof, Wade Clark. *A Generation of Seekers*. New York: Harper and Row, 1993.

Seow, C.L. *Ecclesiastes: A New Translation With Introduction and Commentary*. Garden City, N.Y.: Doubleday, 1997.

Vunderink, R.W. "Epicureans." *The International Standard Bible Encyclopedia*. Geoffrey W. Bromiley, ed. Grand Rapids: William B. Eerdmans, 1982. II:20.

White, James Emery. *A Search for the Spiritual*. Grand Rapids: Baker Books, 1998.

Whybray, R.N. *Ecclesiastes*. Grand Rapids: Eerdmans, 1989.

Write, J. Stafford. *The Expositor's Bible Commentary*. Grand Rapids: Zondervan Publishing House, 1991. V:1139-1141.

Young, E. J. *Introduction to the Old Testament*. Grand Rapids: Eerdmans, 1949.

LaVergne, TN USA
06 December 2010
207569LV00002B/1/A